Surrender to God Within

Pathwork at the Soul Level

The Pathwork Series:
General Editor: Donovan Thesenga

The Pathwork of Self-Transformation
Eva Pierrakos
Bantam, 1990. ISBN 0-553-34896-5

Fear No Evil:
The Pathwork Method
of Transforming the Lower Self
Eva Pierrakos and Donovan Thesenga
Pathwork Press, 1993. ISBN 0-9614777-2-5

Creating Union:
The Pathwork of Relationship
Eva Pierrakos and Judith Saly
Pathwork Press, 1993. ISBN 0-9614777-3-3

The Undefended Self:
Living the Pathwork of Spiritual Wholeness
Susan Thesenga
Pathwork Press, 1994. ISBN 0-9614777-4-1

Surrender to God Within:
Pathwork at the Soul Level
Eva Pierrakos and Donovan Thesenga
Pathwork Press, 1997. ISBN 0-9614777-5-X

Published by **Pathwork Press**
1355 Stratford Court, #16, Del Mar, California 92014
ph(619)793-1246 fax(619)259-5224
e-mail: PathPress@aol.com

Surrender to God Within

Pathwork at the Soul Level

by
Eva Pierrakos

Selected and Shaped by
Donovan Thesenga

Pathwork Press
1997

Chapter 4 appeared in different form in *The Pathwork of Self-Transformation*, Bantam, 1990.

Library of Congress Catalog Card Number: 97-68538
Psychology/Self-Help/Spirituality/Pathwork

ISBN 0-9614777-5-X

Cover Design and Book Design: Karen Millnick
Thanks to Donovan and Susan Thesenga, Gene and Peg Humphrey, and the beings in the spiritual realm who oversee the production of the Pathwork books. Thanks to Jerome Domurat for use of his personal library. Thanks to Kemper Conwell.

Cover Artwork: Dr. Dennis Harp
Dr. Harp, Director of National Physics Outreach at Purdue University and Executive Producer of Vikas Productions created this design initially to depict the most recently observed inner nature of an electron. The bright spot in the center represents a "bare" electron. The thin white lines radiating out from it indicate the particle's electric field, and the central reddish glow represents the area most strongly affected by the electron's charge. The blue and gold elipses are virtual particle/antiparticle pairs which blink into and out of existence almost instantaneously.

Quotations by Meister Eckhart are reprinted with permission from *Meditations with Meister Eckhart* by Matthew Fox, Copyright © 1983, Bear & Company, Inc., Santa Fe, New Mexico.

PRINTED IN THE UNITED STATES OF AMERICA

Prologue

Imagine a time when all is one: the time preceding the great explosion that began our universe.

In this time that preceded time, all on the physical plane, all matter and energy, was one. In this time that was the beginning of time, all on the spiritual plane was also one.

Imagine now that the explosion that begins time generates a division from one to many on the physical plane— an impulse that is paralleled by an equally powerful division from unity to multiplicity on the spiritual plane.

Call the physical plane *The Universe*.

Call the spiritual plane *God*.

In the time *after* time began, matter and energy came to seem to be different from each other. The Universe dispersed infinitely. This time after time began also brought forth a state in which the souls of all beings came to seem to be different from each other. God dispersed infinitely.

The great explosion into apparent multiplicity spawned countless apparent dualities. To all outward appearances, human beings live in this world of duality. In this existence on the material plane, we find, for example, that life is opposed to death, and that to be womanly is to be unmanly; that to seek the light is to leave the dark, and up can be down only in dreams.

Now, through the explorations of our physicists, we have come to know that matter and energy are still one, are interchangeable forms. We've learned that no slightest ripple anywhere in the universe fails to affect every other particle of matter and wave of energy everywhere in the universe.

We also know, deep in our souls, that all God pieces are still one in essence, and every move that any one of us may make toward deeper realization of our Godhood affects all other God particles everywhere.

We can understand our journey now as one of moving from original unity to fragmented multiplicity back to *conscious* unity. For although the essential unity of all matter, all energy, and all spirit has never changed, our task as human beings is to build the bridges, do the work necessary to transcend the illusion of being separate and alone. The harvest of this work will be a life lived in a state of consciousness of unity, in the midst of apparent multiplicity.

It is this consciousness of unity that we thirst for, that we seek and can find, in our journey here on earth.

Donovan Thesenga

Contents

Acknowledgments

Jan Fowler read the entire manuscript and made many
suggestions for improvements, helping me especially with
the introductory pieces.

Karen Millnick did loving and thoughtful design work.

Judith Saly contributed the glossary.

Gene Humphrey was a warm and supportive publisher.

Jack Clarke and David Wagner
offered many helpful suggestions.

The trustees of the Pathwork Foundation paid the bills.

Susan Thesenga reassured me often that this labor was indeed
worthwhile and would one day actually be completed.

—Donovan Thesenga

"Pathwork at the Soul Level"

We say on the cover that this is "Pathwork at the Soul Level," and it seems only fair to define what we mean by this.

Spiritual seeking is no longer the province only of wandering pilgrims and solitary monks. Countless ordinary people have embarked upon a journey to know themselves more deeply, and to learn from experience how to enrich their lives from the inside out. For most people the conscious goal is, at first, simply to learn how to feel better and how to live a more effective and fulfilling life. Those who are involved in the inner search have already learned that this is to be accomplished not by earning more money or by exchanging one's current spouse for a better one, but rather by exploring more deeply our minds and our feelings — our beliefs, hopes, dreams, misconceptions and fears.

So we struggle to find the therapy that fits, find the path that leads where we need to go. The great and wonderful variety of current paths and therapies is a testament to the diversity of human beings and the courage of their search. Suppose that in time we do find that our efforts have borne fruit and we truly do learn to know ourselves more deeply, and a greater degree of wisdom and happiness follows. What then? Some may choose to stop there. Others sense that their path still continues.

After what is often many years of self-work, the seeker comes to a threshold leading to an entirely new way of working. Crossing this threshold requires a profound shift of perspective, not just in the work but in our entire conception of self. At this point the work becomes more specifically *spiritual*, and it requires learning a new relationship to the concept and the experience of *surrender*. We will be exploring this threshold and the shift it calls forth in us.

This book, then, *is not primarily about **personal growth*** in the usual sense. It is not about dissolving neuroses or improving the personality. The shift into surrender is not primarily an emotional process, and does not involve getting more in touch with one's feelings. It has little or nothing to do with healing childhood hurts.

What is this work then? It is learning how to surrender to God and to the will of God. It is learning how to *align* with God. It is learning how to get all of my molecules, all my thoughts and feelings into harmony with the Divine. This is a *spiritual* work, as opposed to psychological or emotional. This book is intended for those who have already done a great deal of work on these prior levels and who are now ready for the next step.

In a sense, this book is a paradoxical invitation to let go of any such previous work; which is not to discount the importance of such preparation, for learning how to disconnect from our damaging neuroses and how to claim more wisdom and happiness are noble goals and essential prerequisites. The work involved in attaining these goals has undoubtedly involved serious effort in examining and transforming inner blocks and distortions, and making the necessary accompanying outer changes in our lives and habits.

The premise we are exploring here, however, is that true spiritual work requires a complete shift of perspective. It brings a radical new understanding of self and world that is not always comfortable or satisfying, that may not even yield, for a long time to come, pleasant outer results. Spiritual work means fearlessly giving up any goals or expectations —even cherished ones like finding a mate or improving our health—and simply surrendering to God's will. This surrendering needs a foundation of mental and emotional health that may indeed be hard-won. But the work of surrender takes place at a new, different level, in faith that this alone, not any desires or agendas of "little me," is what will henceforth guide and empower our lives.

I wish to stress that this is a *radical* shift of emphasis and direction. It is possible that you might read this book once and falsely believe that you fully understand it. But then, as your path continues, you will probably have the experience, more than once, of dropping through what you thought was a floor and feeling lost and ungrounded for quite some time until you find a new floor. Or, to change the metaphor, you may find that you arrive at what you assumed would be the ultimate goal, only to find, at the top of the mountain, that a vast new range of mountains to climb can only now be seen.

Stages on the Path

It is often helpful to think of this inner work as occurring in stages or cycles. The work often begins by paying attention to the level of the child self: healing old hurts, redeeming painful childhood episodes. Once the child self is stronger and freer, the growth process can proceed with work to strengthen the adult ego, helping it to learn its proper role without being over-dominant. Since we are whole organisms, with all aspects of ourselves connected, it is also crucial to engage in some kind of process to relax and enliven the physical body. Then the work moves "out" from the solely individual and becomes focused on fostering harmony and reality in one's human relationships and with non-human life and the earth.

It should be noted that the process that anyone goes through in healing and transforming the self is never this linear or systematic. Some aspects of our personal work seem to come fairly easily, while other areas of more severe distortion and pain may resurface and need attention for years. However, the overall scheme presented here outlines a progression of healing and alignment that seems representative of many people's experiences.

The Leap to the Soul Level

It is only after we have made good headway in integrating and harmonizing our human and earthly relationships that work at the soul or transpersonal level can commence. This is a qualitatively different kind of work. Up to now we have worked primarily at the level of "selves." Now we begin to explore who we are at levels *beyond* the familiar, discrete self that we've been so focused on trying to heal. Instead of working more on who we *are*, we now need to work on *not* being a contained, discrete me—not because this is nobler or grander, but because this is *required* in order to understand and interact with the levels of reality we will now encounter. If we respond to this invitation to sacrifice the little self, we are repaid a thousand fold, with the emergence of our real self. From our real self we can build and feel our connections with the infinite love and wisdom of spiritual reality. As we surrender to this vast reality more and more, we enter a state of oneness and unity.

The Pathwork

The material gathered here was originally in the form of lectures, delivered by Eva Pierrakos, and designed for verbal presentation rather than for reading. Eva delivered 258 such lectures, spread over the course of twenty-two years. These concepts attracted hundreds and then thousands of people, and the manner of applying and working with these ideas came to be known as "the Pathwork." There is now a worldwide network of Pathwork centers and groups in North and South America, Europe, and Australia.

Three previous volumes of Pathwork lectures have been published, dealing with the psychological and emotional levels of the work. This book is concerned with the nature of spiritual reality, the ways that the spiritual and material interact, and who we are at the level of the transpersonal.

Much of the wisdom to be found in this volume contradicts common sense, but this is to be expected. To enter upon and keep moving along a true path of spiritual realization means to be deeply surprised, over and over again. We hope that you will allow these surprises, be open and porous, and let a different state of consciousness emerge as you read.

Introduction Two

How to Use This Book

I arranged this book with an eye to its flow from beginning to end, but it is not necessary to read it in sequence from start to finish. Feel free to let your intuition draw you to the chapter that will be right in the moment. Over time I assume you will read every chapter and will read some of them many times.

The ideas presented in Part One are "lighter" than those which appear later, and their principal purpose is to introduce you to the spirit of this teaching, to set the stage, as it were. I think you will enjoy these lectures and benefit from them, but reading them is not *essential* for an understanding of the rest of the book.

The principal theoretical statement of *Surrender to God Within* is made in the Introduction to Part Three, "The Great Transition from Self-Centeredness to Love." If you would like to begin with a summary of what this book is all about, its principal contribution to the understanding of the spiritual path, you might choose to begin by reading this section first.

Many of the chapters contain specific recommendations for practice, various awareness exercises, and different uses for the meditative state. I urge you to *practice* these, rather than simply to understand them and then go on reading.

The Pathwork lectures use some words, such as "image" or "real self," in a specific, somewhat untraditional manner. Since this volume may be the first Pathwork book you have read, I have included a glossary that defines these terms and should help you to understand the concepts more thoroughly.

The lectures I have chosen for this volume span a great length of time, from 1957, the first year that Eva began this work, to 1979 when she died. However, the tone and the message stay remarkably consistent. I made many choices along the way about what to include and what to leave out, in the process of turning this material into a book. The idea of gathering together the Pathwork teachings pertaining to spirituality and surrender, and the work of editing and assembling these teachings, writing the introductory passages, and choosing a title, was mine.

I hope that Eva's work and my own blend together into a whole, and that this whole nourishes you along your path to full realization.

Donovan Thesenga
Sevenoaks
Madison, Virginia
July, 1996

Part One

The Spirit World

" The eye with which I see God is
the same eye with which God sees me."
—*Meister Eckhart*

The three lectures in this section are among the earliest delivered by Eva Pierrakos. They describe complex spiritual truths in
a style that is simultaneously challenging and approachable.

Several concepts appear here that are repeatedly interwoven
through the body of the Pathwork material. One is that we, in
this incarnation and many others, have come to earth with a
particular mission, a task of purification and transformation.
The real self carries with it into incarnation aspects of separated
consciousness that must be brought into union so that universal love can flourish. Furthermore, this task *must* be done on
earth, with its suffering, injustice and apparent imperfections.
It is only in this environment that the imperfections in *us* that
need attention can surface and offer themselves to be healed.
When we sincerely take in and learn to have faith in this truth,
we are blessed with joy and vast understanding.

Another central teaching is the importance — the absolute
necessity — of looking into all aspects of ourselves, particularly
those parts that we might not like. It is only in fearlessly exposing and accepting the negative in us that we can transform and
free the energy that it has been holding. The power of this goes
far beyond the merely therapeutic. Revealing our dark and
destructive currents not only helps us begin to heal our personality — it also lifts us into the realm where we can begin to
surrender our personality and align totally with the Divine. We are
assured that the more we undertake this often difficult and painful
work, the more help we receive from those in the spirit world who
constantly guide us toward the fulfillment of our task.

We invite you to proceed with an open mind and trusting
heart as we begin our immersion in the Pathwork teachings.

D.T.

CHAPTER 1

The Kingdom of God
Is Within

I greet you in God's name, my dear friends. I bring you blessings.

It is difficult to understand the real meaning of the teaching that the Kingdom of God is within. You imagine that this refers to a mood and therefore to some unreal thing that cannot be grasped. People only take for real what they can see and touch; feeling states cannot be seen or touched. When I explain to you that thoughts and feelings are forms, it may become somewhat easier for you to understand that these forms build corresponding spheres and landscapes. This explanation, however, still may not make it clear how all this can exist within. Human beings believe that there is no space within for landscapes and spheres, and difficult as it is to explain this with words, I still want to try to lead you to further insight into spiritual states.

Just as time on earth is entirely different from its true reality in spirit, so it is with space also. Spatial dimensions like above, below, right, or left are concepts that you can grasp in your early habitat, but they do not exist in that way in the spiritual dimension. When human beings divest themselves of their bodies, they go inward into the spiritual worlds, because the whole universe is actually within the human being. This is a fact.

Maybe you can understand this concept if I give you an example, however insufficient: Think of opera glasses into which you look from the wrong end so that everything becomes very small. This little picture will be the reality according to your limited understanding. Now you might pose the question how the entire universe, with its vast size, could exist in every human being. I would answer you in the following manner: Your earthly world is not the actual reality, not even in a figurative, symbolic sense; it is only a reflection, an image in a mirror, a projection of the real.

The Realness of Inner Reality

I wish to stress again: When I speak of inner reality in this context I do not merely refer to a psychological or emotional state. The inner reality is the wide, vast universe. You as a personality stand on the borderline. On one side is this wide, vast, endless, infinite inner space of divine creation, in which every conceivable state of consciousness, expression, and condition exists; and on the other side is the outer void that has to be filled with consciousness and light, with love and life. Your material body is the boundary, the border state. The consciousness behind the body is the carrying agent whose task it is to bring one's inner reality into the void. The only difficulty is that those in this border state often forget that the inner reality is the real world, or even that there is such a world beyond the realm of matter.

The darkness of the limited mind makes it almost impossible to conceive of an actual world existing within or through you that leads to reflected reality. Only the space of the three-dimensional state of consciousness appears real. Yet even your physicists today know that the relationship of time/space/movement is of an infinite variety, and therefore the time/space/movement continuum of the world of your state of consciousness is relative and only one of many possibilities, rather than a fixed, exclusive "reality" applicable to all inner states. When a human consciousness "dies," as it were, what actually happens is that it withdraws from its shell into another time/space/movement continuum, which is the inner world.

Being in the body, which houses the spirit, brings about a separation. The moment the separating wall falls because you leave your body behind, the universe that exists in every single human being unifies — of course *on condition* that you have developed yourself far enough to reach the spheres where there is no longer any separation. The lower the sphere in which an entity finds itself — be it in the here and now or in the beyond — the more radical must be the separation.

Just as time, space, and the relationship of movement to time and space within your specific reality are results of a corresponding state of consciousness, so are landscapes, objects, conditions, natural laws, the atmosphere, and the climate also results of specific states of consciousness. Your inner world is thus a total product of your overall state of consciousness. In this inner world you connect with others whose overall state of consciousness approximates your own, so that you share a commonly created sphere of temporary reality. This same rule applies, of course, to this earth sphere, with the only difference being that the inner states are externalized on earth in a way that often makes it more difficult to discern the inner reality.

You also know that your own consciousness is not just one unified state. You consist of many aspects of consciousness which may often be in total disagreement among themselves and whose state of development may vary widely.

The Real Self Chooses a Task

When the *real self*[1] takes on a task before it goes into an embodiment, it chooses to take certain aspects of consciousness along with it, if I may put it this way. On the path you are helped to fulfill this task which your real self understood, which is to bring unification between the disconnected aspects of your consciousness, and also to refine, reeducate, and purify these divergent aspects. Your ego, which is your active, determining outer consciousness, can choose to seek an understanding of these connections, or to evade it. Your ego consciousness is the borderline between the inner light world and the outer void. As I said, when the human mind becomes entangled in the partial reality of three-dimensional consciousness, it can easily forget the task. Only through a struggle can it be reawakened to the greater consciousness. I might also add here that human beings receive a great deal of spiritual guidance in this struggle if only they are willing to perceive the help.

When the disconnected mind forgets the greater truth of being, the conscious ego self temporarily identifies with the aspects needing reeducation and purification; it then loses a sense of its real identity. This extremely painful state comes about only when pride, self-will, and fear are allowed to rule the consciousness. The moment you have exposed, owned, and realistically evaluated those negative aspects you had exclusively identified with and therefore struggled against seeing, this shameful isolation ceases and the aspects are seen exactly for what they are: simply aspects of the total self.

It is therefore extremely important in your Pathwork that you explore yourself and stop hiding the negative part of yourself. For the more you hide it, the more you lose yourself

---

1. See Glossary for definition of **Real Self**.

in it and the greater the desperation of the illusion becomes. Only when you take the courage and adopt the humility to again and again acknowledge and expose the negative parts of yourself does the miracle occur: you will then no longer secretly identify with those parts of you which you wish to hide. Paradoxical as this may seem at first glance, the more you expose your destructive part, the more you know your beauty; the more you expose your inner hatred and all its derivatives, the more you know of your already existing state of love that can then shine through.

Exposing the Lower Reveals the Higher

Just imagine, my friends, the incredibly painful predicament you put yourself in when you hide that which you are most ashamed and afraid of. It is precisely because of this hiding that you compound the very attitudes you most hate in yourself. You make them infinitely worse through the concealment, and then you become more and more convinced on deep levels of your consciousness that they constitute your real being. This *vicious circle* [2] makes you more determined to hide and therefore you feel more isolated, more negative, and more destructive just because of your methods of hiding. For hiding always requires projecting your real guilt onto others, blaming, whitewashing the self, hypocrisy, and so on. Therefore you become more convinced that the hidden part is the ultimate you for whom there is no hope. Your true task must begin by exposing all of you. I have said it so many times, because there just is no way around this aspect of spiritual development. All the seekers of spiritual growth who avoid this delude themselves and must at one time or another encounter a rude and painful awakening. You must go through this process; you must expose all parts. Yet such an exposure also brings in its wake the awareness that the worst opinion of yourself is never justified, no matter how ugly the traits and attitudes may be that you have hidden. They are never justified because these parts are only isolated aspects of the total consciousness which your real self has taken charge of.

As you go through these steps, you become aware of your higher self, not as a theory or a philosophical premise, but as simple reality, right here and now. You experience yourself as the real entity you are, have always been and will always be, no matter what the isolated aspects of consciousness fabricate in

2. See Glossary for definition of **Vicious Circle**.

the way of delusion and folly. This is indeed a great and wonderful task! In the process you learn about your inner reality and all its various aspects and levels of consciousness. You see the outer event in relation to your inner landscape. The inner landscape is then no longer some symbolic or colorful analogy. It is indeed *stark* reality.

The Soul's Journey

The analogy often used in dreams as well as in other symbolic language is that one's sojourn in a human body is a journey. This analogy reveals a profound truth: the inner path is in constant movement through the stages of soul matter that have to be traversed. This journey is indeed not just a word. It is a constant flowing movement. And so is your own personal path. It is a movement. It carries you through your landscapes. It carries you to the landscape of your higher self, which is beautiful and brilliant. But if the task you have come to fulfill is left behind, you will not experience this beautiful landscape too often, because you get stuck and stay in the landscapes of those other aspects of your consciousness which you have not yet united and integrated with the real self.

What happens when you withdraw after a lifetime into the inner universe with these various aspects of your personality? You live in them alternately. The aspects you have not succeeded in unifying with the higher self remain separated fragments in their own self-created worlds. You must occasionally reside in these separate worlds; the amount of "time," for lack of a better word, depends on the intensity of each state. Each will indeed be a world like this material world, for example, but with different conditions, dimensions, and laws which appear to be the only reality for as long as your mind is fixed on them, just as this sphere seems the only reality while you are exclusively focused on it. All these worlds are worlds of consciousness and action. Since you have many different aspects, you will reside in many different worlds. While your consciousness is focused on any of these other worlds, you forget your real identity; you function just as a human being does, not knowing your real divine identity as long as you only identify with the less-developed aspects of your being. Then indeed the sojourn in the lower worlds of those aspects seems final for as long as it lasts. This finality is an illusion, but only when you are in the greater reality of your light world do you know that the only final reality is beauty, love, truth, light, and bliss. All other states are temporary.

Beyond a certain level of development every single spiritual being reaches a stage of purification where it is capable of surrendering to the divine flow, dissolving itself, and melting into it. And it can also reconstitute these fluid threads so that it again becomes an entity of form and shape, although of such fine substance that beings who have not yet reached a high state of development cannot perceive it.

Everyone can experience a faint echo of this blissful feeling of melting into oneness when overtaken by a feeling of immense bliss. You can perhaps sense how much longing there is in you to dissolve the self, not only in the union of love, but also in all the great experiences of the soul when it is lifted high and close to God, in whatever way this may happen— through nature, music, meditation, or simply when the breath of God touches the human being. Then you really feel that your body limits you, and you wish to break the limits so that you can surrender to the stream and mingle with it. Perhaps you have never thought in these terms, but you probably will confirm that at times you have known such feelings.

The less purified the soul is — and I do not refer only to faults and weaknesses but also to anxieties and unhealthy currents — the more the person fears self-surrender, in spite of yearning for it. The more spiritualized the soul, the less it will resist the surrender. Some human philosophies have actually grasped this. Through such insight, these philosophies have come to the conclusion that this state is the final destination of humanity. However, this is not true. Although there is a melting and dissolving, the individuality, the "I" - consciousness is not lost. Again and again, those beings will contract the fluidal threads and from the state of pure *being* move into the state of *doing*. In the stage of doing one has to become a complete and harmonious form. And since God is creator — that is, doer,— this process takes place within God as well. The active element of God that creates contracts over and over again into the purest and most perfect form. Thus the element of God that simply is and sustains, consequently also dissolves itself. These concepts are extremely difficult for you human beings to integrate into your understanding, but I hope my words can spark a flash of insight.

I am explaining a contradiction that is inherent in human understanding. It also touches on the subject of dualism and monism. People who have had a God-experience in the state of being, in the state of dissolution, suppose that is the only and final truth. Others, however, who have experienced God in the other manifestation, as form, as creator, believe that this is the ultimate truth. Here is the origin of the contradiction, and I tell you that both God-experiences are equally true.

Are there any questions?

QUESTION: You have explained to us that our reality is only a mirror of the true reality. I cannot understand this. When we touch a tree, for example, the bark is so real to us.

ANSWER: It is just as difficult to clarify this as to understand it. And if you cannot grasp it today, that does not matter. Later —maybe in one or two or five years — suddenly a light will be shed on the problem. You will have an inkling, a sense of what it means. Then these words will affect you in a very different way.

Certainly, what you touch is real or seems to you real. When you touch a mirror, that is also real. You feel the mirror. Let us assume you do not know that the living being reflected in the mirror is warm, and blood flows in its veins, and thus you do not know how that being is actually experienced in touch. You could then mistake the mirror image for the real person. Imagine the relationship between the two realities somewhat like this. You do not know how anything in the reality of which you are not conscious feels to the touch, looks to the eye, and sounds to the ear. For you, the ultimate criterion is in touching, hearing or seeing, because you have no basis of comparison and, for now, you lack higher spiritual perception.

And now I shall withdraw, giving God's blessings to each one of you. May God's love strengthen you, open you up, and guide you to spiritual growth.

CHAPTER 2

Choosing Your Destiny

I bring you God's blessings, my dear ones.

When an entity undertakes to incarnate into another life on earth, it brings to it the tasks it has to fulfill; the plan is outlined. And in many cases the spirit itself has the right to discuss its future life with those spirit beings whose responsibility this is: thus the incarnating entity can contribute — to a certain extent, according to its already acquired vision and capacity to judge —as to how its destiny will unfold. For in the spirit state the entity has a wider view than when housed in a body and understands that the purpose of life is not to have it as comfortable as possible, but to develop toward a higher state, to reach perfect bliss as rapidly as possible — a state that does not exist on earth. The entity knows that only through spiritual effort can its spiritual knowledge penetrate its intellect; but it also knows that it cannot easily achieve this, and that, once incarnated, difficulties, tests, and even so-called disasters are often necessary to lead one to the right path and the right attitude.

Memory fades automatically the moment matter envelops the spirit. This is essential, for spiritual awareness has to be fought for, and this can happen only when one takes the trouble to search within the self —not only outside and in general terms —for God and the truths of Creation. Only within one's own soul can one recognize the very special meaning and purpose of one's life, together with the individual tasks that one has to fulfill. However, those who constantly allow themselves to be impressed by the outward aspects of life on earth lose this inner meaning, and sometimes they have to go through life after life without much progress, incarnating again and again for the same purpose.

The spirit knows the danger of earthly life, but knows also that if one lives life in the right way from the spiritual point of view, one can develop on earth disproportionately faster than in the spirit world, exactly because it is easier there. The difficulties on earth are mainly connected with matter and all that this implies. This is so partly because the memory of the spirit realm has been extinguished and needs to be regained, and partly because matter contains so much temptation. Only those who overcome these difficulties can win and make the best of their lives on earth. The spirits about to be incarnated know that they need hardship to shake them into wakefulness so that they do not get imprisoned in matter and in all that matter attracts to it. Before incarnation, therefore, a spirit may ask the higher beings: "I beg you, help me, not only with your strength and guidance, but also, when you see that I am not fulfilling myself, send me tests and trials, for when these come I have a better chance to wake up and look at my life from a different point of view than when everything functions regularly and without friction."

So it is important for you to recognize that many of the events in your life which seem to repeat themselves were chosen and planned by you when you still had your wider vision, before matter enveloped your spirit. It will be helpful for you to know this. A very ambitious spirit may sometimes even ask for a particularly difficult destiny, knowing clearly in the state of freedom from matter that the pain to be suffered is little and of short duration in comparison to the gain. This should give you food for thought.

I suggest to each one of you, my friends, to think about your life and your trials and tribulations. Ask whether they could not have been chosen by yourselves to make sure you do not remain unaware of something that you should fulfill. Contemplate from this viewpoint what you should still find and solve within you. If you search for it with your entire will, the answer will be given to you, you will sense it, you will be given insights. This, too, has to be learned; it needs practice. Do not believe that the ability to meditate will come by itself. It needs willpower, perseverance; you have to fight your negative currents. But the reward is great and truly blissful; the effort is worth it. When the spirit world recognizes that a person does this with sincere good will, then guidance will be given also from the outside, to help you achieve what you intend.

When a spirit realizes, after life is over and it has discarded the material shell, that it has not fulfilled everything that had been planned, it is often allowed in the spirit state to bring the past incarnation to completion to finish tasks already begun and shed some burdens. One can then continue to be involved with his family or whatever group of people he had intended to accomplish a task with, only as a spirit it is much more difficult. It is easier in the sense that clear vision is restored, the extinguished memory regained, and one understands what it is all about, but it is more difficult because the possibility of working effectively is much reduced as a spirit.

For instance, a living person can influence another especially effectively by overcoming his or her own faults. Indirect influence is always effective and lasting. Example is always more convincing than words, persuasion, or forcing one's will upon the other, no matter how right or well-intentioned one is. To the degree you overcome your own weaknesses, affirm the spiritual laws within yourself, and learn to love, you will get closer to your fellow humans where you need it. It must be so according to spiritual lawfulness. This is indirect influence, but eventually the result becomes evident to everyone. However, as a discarnate spirit you cannot do this, for most people are not open to receive what a spirit is trying to convey through inspiration; even when they perceive it, they often misinterpret or forget it, so it is much more difficult and takes much longer for anyone as a spirit to finish the task begun on earth — if it can be accomplished at all. One may still need another earthly life for this purpose.

Thus every human being and every spirit erects the world in which he or she lives. You build your home in the spirit world after your life on earth, and you build your future life on earth. Every act, thought, feeling has its form, which then builds the spiritual home —even though only temporarily —as well as the fated events of the future incarnation. All this represents not only the natural outcome of the person's individual attitude and outlook, but the spiritual forms so constructed indicate exactly what this entity needs for its further development.

Meditate on these words, for they contain much. They again exemplify that the equation must always come out right: Hardship is self-created, yet precisely because of that, it contains the only medicine there is. Through this you can fathom the vastness of divine wisdom in its magnificent lawfulness. Whoever understands this will also understand that destiny and free will are not two mutually exclusive factors, but are interwoven and connected. The events that fate brings to you are spiritual forms which have to manifest in a concrete way. If through ignorance of these laws unfavorable forms are created, each being has to dissolve them himself, and this can happen only by entering a spiritual path of inner discipline, self-knowledge, and self-search.

The Will to Change

For all this you need willpower. Many of you, my friends, will say: "That's all very well, but one person is born with a strong portion of willpower, and another is not. So how can someone who hasn't got any willpower make use of it?" Let me explain.

Willpower, just as any other quality, has to be engendered and built up by yourself. It cannot be otherwise. A person born with a strong will must have worked to acquire it some time in the past, so he or she could bring this valuable possession —if I may call it that —along, and now it can be put to good use. If this hasn't happened yet, the person should work for it in this incarnation. The same holds true for all the other qualities, whether it is the capacity to love, to have tolerance, kindliness, or anything else. And I would like to show you how each one of you can acquire willpower. For God never asks for the impossible from anyone, my dear ones, ever.

Willpower is a direct result of understanding, of knowledge, and of the corresponding decision. For every human being has a certain amount of strength, and it is entirely up to him or her in what direction to channel it. Many people waste this strength either in useless efforts which build nothing that is of spiritual value, or they give over to sick, unpurified emotional currents. These use up much energy. It is yet another spiritual law that energy used for spiritually positive goals is always replenished. But when your strength is caught up in negative circles of spiritually unproductive currents, it gets depleted and wasted because it cannot be renewed, at least not sufficiently.

This is why you see so often that people who do a lot of good seem to have superhuman strength. Those who know what life is all about will channel the energy at their disposal wisely and reset the inner switches accordingly. When one just drifts along, without giving a thought to the true meaning of life, much of the energy will go into false channels and thus be used up without sufficient renewal. Thus the first step toward willpower is meditation. Because for someone who has gained a certain understanding, it will be easier to draw the relevant inner conclusions and to make the outward decisions that follow from them.

It is a decision and an inner reorientation when a person can say: "Well, I live here on earth for a certain reason. Maybe I lack the willpower to fulfill the purpose of my existence as well as it could be possible by overcoming all my resistances, but I will ask God for this willpower, for basically I do want what is good. I will take the time and the little effort to reflect upon these things and open myself to divine enlightenment and devote regularly, daily, twenty to thirty minutes to my spiritual life. And when I find that at first I still lack the willpower, then I will take this problem into my meditation, into my dialogue with God and thus help my still weak willpower to grow."

Everybody can do that. This much willpower, this much self-discipline is available to everyone. You do not have to start with what is most difficult; after all, you do not start with the roof when you build a house, but with the foundation. The idea is to shift the energy and the emphasis. When a person finally makes this decision and abides by it —a decision that is not too difficult or too much for anyone —then the spirit world will also help to strengthen his or her willpower, so that the further and actually more difficult steps of development will seem much easier. I can promise this to you, my friends, and some of you can already confirm that it is so. And thus even the person who initially was lacking in willpower will, in due course, have just as much as those who were born with it.

The Will to Meditate

Those who understand what is at stake and to what area to shift their main concentration, and who bring this understanding from a superficial intellectual level into deeper levels, will be able to take the necessary decisive step. It happens through the regular practice of the correct meditation, which of course has to be learned as part of this path. The decision to develop your willpower has to be made at one time or another. To summarize: To obtain willpower you have to, first, gain understanding and, second, make the decision that follows from it. Therefore, if you feel that you don't have enough willpower, you lack the illuminating understanding of what it is all about. Yes, you may have a vague sense of the meaning of willpower, but your soul is not yet penetrated by it, maybe because something in you resists and clings to the comfortable, undisciplined old attitude. You are then split inside. One part has some spiritual knowledge, yet the other part does not draw the conclusions from what you feel "sort of vaguely." This is why the first step must be to deepen the superficial knowledge, to work on that first, so that the whole personality is penetrated by understanding. When you do this first —and you can if you take a little trouble and time —you will certainly make the decision and have the willpower to direct your life and your energies toward the spiritual, recognizing and fully understanding that *only* in this way can you also solve the problems in your earthly life. And this is how a person creates within the self such a powerful energy that all the subsequent steps upward on the path will become easier and easier. As always, and in everything, the beginning is the most difficult.

From our perspective, we often observe that people who believe they do not have enough willpower would have it if they directed their available energies into the right channel, if they would only reset the switch. But only the insight into the necessity of this change will make you act. As long as you deceive yourself into believing that you can manage without it, you will not act but will amble along as before. The pursuit of a path that seems comfortable, however, means that the relationship to God is not entirely harmonious. Whoever meditates and reflects upon these things in this way will have to arrive at the right conclusion and will have to make the right decision, so that life becomes a living religion and not just a theory.

Do you think that we expect too much of you? Is it too much to devote a little time and effort every day to look into yourself, to find the areas where something is lacking, so as to improve your spiritual awareness? And when the willpower is not there and it is so difficult to muster a daily discipline, then, after asking for help, search into yourself to find what it is that hinders you so much. If you are afraid that you might find something that you would much rather keep buried, then you will benefit from using simple, healthy logic, which will tell you that nothing can remain hidden from God and the realm of spirit — and not even from yourself, once you return to that world. And the sooner it surfaces, the better for you and the easier to deal with. For you know that what is hidden brings far greater conflicts than what is out in the open, recognized, and integrated. Your psychologists know this, too, so that you are quite aware of the fact that you gain nothing when you close your eyes to that which is in you. Think about this deeply, so that the knowledge takes root in your soul. It will be to your greatest benefit.

When you have overcome the initial difficulties and have won some mastery over yourself, at least in this respect, then the spirit world will show you the next step on your path, what has to be worked out and fought for. Life will present it to you. When you have learned to meditate in the right way, you will know how to view every event of your daily life with open eyes, so that you understand its messages.

Even those friends who have overcome the initial difficulties do not always use their quiet hour in the best way. They meditate too often in general terms, always in the same way, not only when praying for other people, but also for themselves. Your meditations and prayers must vary; you need to sense the next step of your development, and when you are not aware of it, the insight will be given if you search honestly, turning your eyes toward what has to be recognized, learned, overcome, and accepted. Take the specific problem of finding your path's direction to God and to Christ, and to your personal spirit friends who are so close to you and whose task it is to help you with it. In this way your prayers will come alive. Then, after you have asked for help to recognize your problems and for the strength to solve them, be still and listen into yourself, and let your thoughts surface and allow them to lead you intuitively. After a while the connections will become clear. You will know where the problem comes from, why you react the way you do, and the increasing awareness of your inner currents will help you forward.

Again and again make the resolution to face your inner truth with courage. Cultivate truthful thoughts: Think everything through clearly, independently. Thus your spiritual life will become more productive, because it will be alive, and therefore also constantly changing. It will not be according to a rigid formula which is repeated daily. And so your relationship to God will unfold toward harmony.

Think about my words, which I was permitted to give to you today. They should take you a little further on your path. And then we have also fulfilled our task.

We spirits who work here rejoice when we see that these words bring you a little closer to God, to your real self, to your happiness and to your inner harmony. Receive the blessings of salvation, may they penetrate you. Go with God, go in peace. God be with you.

CHAPTER 3

Happiness as a Link in the Chain of Life

Greetings. I bring you God's blessings.

God's spirit world would want nothing more than to help you grow spiritually —into happiness, harmony, and light. God's spirits try continually to extend their helping hand to bring you over those hurdles where you are struggling with the difficulties in your spiritual development on this path toward perfection. We can only help, however; we cannot force. First you will have to want to reach perfection, and open the door through wanting it. Only then will you perceive this help as a palpable reality. This, in turn, will increase your feelings of security and deepen your trust in the reality and truthfulness of God's spirit world. Yet it is only too often that humans will pay no attention to the heavenly spirits around them and so will not see, hear, and feel those who offer their help. Even if they believe in principle in the existence of God, they do not think that this has an effect on their personal lives with all their problems. Thus they close the door and may continue walking on a wrong path. Going in the wrong direction often begins with a seemingly trivial choice, but the more one moves away from the point of choice, the farther one will stray into a dead-end street from where it will be ever more difficult to find the way out.

Even when people love God and want the good, they so often do not see in themselves what is the determining factor in their development and fulfillment. What appears to be an unimportant detail is often the root of all unhealthy currents in the soul. You, however, do not recognize it because you are unwilling to awaken to the inspiration coming from the divine spirits. For it always seems more comfortable to stay in the old way. The result is sadness or dissatisfaction with life; you do not understand why, but this is very often the reason, my dear friends.

It is my task to give you hints, to awaken you. May each of you hear what applies to you personally —but even for this the willingness has to be there. Only when you feel it can you absorb and assimilate this material.

Selfish Goals

Whenever human beings set themselves a goal — whether consciously or just emotionally — and this goal is a selfish one, they will often not be able to reach what they want. Even if they reach it, its effect and the satisfaction it gives will be a fleeting one; it will dry out, become shallow, and eventually dissolve. If you want happiness just for yourself, then you will not become happy. Most likely you will say, "But of course I do not want happiness only for myself. I will be very glad to see my fellow human beings also happy." But it makes a great difference whether this is just an occasional and rather superficial thought, formed out of a sense of duty, or whether the wish penetrates your whole being. Each one of you can look inside to ascertain how deep the wish really is. For here too you may deceive yourself; here too you can want something with your mind, but another part of your personality, which I call the lower self, pulls your emotions into quite a different direction. This part does not really care for the other person —not emotionally —and this is the crux of the matter. Almost anybody, unless still on a very low level of development, will in theory feel glad when good things happen to another. But even quite developed people, if honest, often detect in themselves some envy, or a slightly malicious joy over the misfortune of others.

How far along is any individual in this respect? Are you willing to give something up for the sake of another? Ask yourself: "Do I want happiness for my own sake, or is this the second consideration?" Can you go to God and say, "Of course I cannot fool you, just as I cannot fool myself. True, I want to be happy. But when I obtain this happiness, I want to maintain it by becoming a link. What I receive from you I wish to convey to others in some form, even if I have to make a sacrifice —perhaps to renounce my ego-gratification. Please show me how I can give out to others all that I have received from you." If you immerse yourself again and again into this thought, until it takes root in your soul, until it becomes such a powerful spiritual form that it penetrates your entire being on the deepest level of your feelings, then you will have fulfilled the conditions. Then the particular spiritual law can manifest itself through you, and then you will be truly happy, exactly because your own happiness is no longer the ultimate goal of your endeavors. That is, the "I" will give up its self-importance for the sake of the "Thou." Then you seek happiness not only because you want it; on the contrary, the goal will be to give happiness to the other, to others, and your own happiness will merely be a way station, so to speak.

Your happiness will be given to you so that you can pass it on. Then you will indeed become a link in the chain, which is the sole requisite to keep the stream of happiness alive and flowing. In this way it will never dry out. Whatever the person who serves as such a link gives out will be reciprocated a hundredfold. God will always show you how, in what form, your love and knowledge and happiness can be passed on to others, but first you must have the readiness to do so. Indeed, today, tomorrow, next week, and every day you have to make the resolution to be in readiness; you must consciously conquer your resistance. Do not push it into unconsciousness. Then you must try to translate the readiness into action. And so the spiritual law can begin to fulfill itself in you.

I Will Be a Link in the Chain

Let each and every one of you now think about what particular blessing you enjoy; it may be good health, or spiritual strength, or the happiness and security of a loving relationship. It is different with each one of you. Everybody has received a special treasure from God. And once you have decided, "I will no longer want to be the ultimate goal, but rather a link in the chain," it will be shown to you how you can pass on that which you have received, and you will also be richly rewarded, for that is the law.

At the same time you will not take your gifts and treasures for granted. This is always a sign of spiritual desiccation and causes the gifts you possess to lose their luster because the law of giving and receiving has been violated. If you are a living link in the chain, every one of your gifts will regain its shine, and the joy and pleasure that you had lost will be restored to you.

As with happiness in general, so it is with every one of its components that a person may desire: love, strength, health, freedom — everything. Whatever one wants for one's own sake will dissolve, wither away; whatever is sought for the sake of the other, as a link in the chain, will blossom and flourish — for yourself and for the other.

Take, for instance, the many people who are preoccupied with becoming free. They avoid anything that could bind them. But the same law applies here also: Those who desire freedom for its own sake will find themselves bound on the inner level. On the other hand one who desires freedom to become a link in the chain, to effect some special task for God's plan of salvation and for fellow human beings will blossom in freedom without being bound inside. Giving energy to further the upward development of human consciousness, this person will be free not only on the outer level, but inwardly also. Whoever lusts for freedom out of pure egoism, elevating himself above God and claiming freedom from the spiritual laws, becomes less and less free; the vaunted freedom will turn into bondage, and ultimately he will find himself in fetters. Those who ally themselves with God and God's laws will continually increase their freedom and their independence. This is the immutable law, which cannot be overthrown. God's laws were created in wisdom and love, and those who revolt against them out of defiance and ignorance —either because they cannot as yet understand them or because they do not want to comprehend them for unhealthy emotional reasons —must become increasingly unhappy with the resulting tight inner bondage.

God's Justice

Many people who revolt against human injustice cannot comprehend that God is just in spite of human errors, and that in spirit infallible justice reigns. Spiritual justice makes use of human injustice in order to bring about ultimate justice.

This may appear contradictory to some of you. Nevertheless, this is not so; the equation balances out. I will give you an example. Let us suppose that a criminal who has committed several crimes has gotten away with it every time. He laughs into his beard, both at the stupidity of people, and at the lack of justice, which seems to be to his advantage. Then one day he is arrested for a crime he did not commit. You will find that it is exactly this kind of person who will scream loudest about the injustice in this world. He went scot free all those other times and now, when he is innocent, he is forced to pay. The more obstinate such a person is, the less will he recognize the great justice prevailing over the minor injustice. He will not want to see this. But this is how he is being tested. For it would be all too easy to recognize spiritual justice with all its ramifications if the connection between crime and punishment were always so evident. The imperfection which human beings have created for themselves must be the remedy, so to speak, through which they can regain the lost perfection.

If complete justice reigned on earth —and this in itself is an impossibility, since the imperfection came into being out of free will and has to be overcome through free will —then it would be too simple for you humans: earth would not be a testing ground, and it would be meaningless to strive for the attainment of a higher consciousness. The attaining of a higher state of consciousness is the utmost grace, to which the door must be opened by the entity itself. So you are tested as to whether or not you are willing to see farther, even if this means giving up selfwill, spite, self-righteousness, and other negative currents. The magnitude and glory of God's creation lies exactly in the fact that imperfection is used as a means to attain perfection, that human injustice is used to bring about divine justice.

Now the example I just used is a crass one; nevertheless it applies in one way or another to everybody. If you really want to find out whether this is so in your case, the insight will be given to you, though of course it is not easy to meet yourself so honestly. You often have to pay for something that you have not committed —but what you are really paying for lies buried in the past. What it is can be found out only by summoning the inner will in meditation. And even if the action for which you have to pay now was committed in a past life, the insight can come, provided you follow this path of development and purification. Helpful insights are given by heaven as a result of your honest endeavors, for your humility and goodwill.

It can also happen that you are not asked to account for a series of smaller trespasses. The spirit world is willing to wait and see whether you will conclude on your own that something in your character needs to be improved. But if you do not search in this direction, the effect of all the neglected deviations will descend upon you, as it were, in one fell swoop; you will have to pay off all the little things. This may make it easier to awaken you to the fact that you have to change something in yourself. And here again your attitude will be tested. Will you say, "I never did anything wrong enough to justify all that is coming to me now," or will you assume that God cannot be unjust and therefore begin to explore whatever it is in you that needs to be uncovered? This is always the question, and your answer makes all the difference as to whether you are passing the test or not; it will determine the direction of your development.

It is a special grace — and I purposely choose this word — when you can pay off your violations of spiritual law in the same life and not in the next, since it is so much easier to see the connecting threads and thus recognize ultimate justice, even when it comes in a roundabout way. Such experiences will make you feel that there is safe ground under your feet and establish your permanent trust in God. But, as I said, the grace of recognition can be given to you even if what you pay off reaches back into a previous incarnation, provided you are absolutely determined to choose self-awareness and purification. In this way it will be easier for you to harmonize your relationship to God. And harmony with God brings about your happiness. I tell you all this so that you can think about your difficulties and find out whether you are paying for something that you caused in this life or in a previous one. Whichever it is, you can still find the seed in you; it must be a special fault which has to be recognized and dealt with.

Opening the Unconscious

When humans shed their body and enter the realm of spirit, most of what you call the unconscious is open and accessible. Not one of you, my dear ones, not even those who have already progressed on this path or who are actually in a state of healing, have even the remotest idea of the reality of this unconscious, which is so often deeply split into opposing currents and works against the conscious mind. Some of those who are in healing may have caught a glimpse of it. Encountering these previously unconscious currents and tendencies feels as if you met a total stranger who leads his own life. It requires work, discipline, and training to feel into these currents and recognize precisely what they are. The encounter with this stranger is a sign of great progress; you have every reason to rejoice. Sing "Glory Hallelujah." For the first battle is won, the first step toward the unification of your personality has been taken.

It is a great mistake to believe that if you do not look at the undercurrents, their effect will be less severe. You know by now that all thoughts and feelings create spiritual forms of the greatest reality, even if you cannot see them. These forms have far-reaching effects: In ever-spreading circles, actions create reactions, which again have consequences, so that a long chain reaction ensues. You may control some of the outermost manifestations of the long chain, but this is not enough. Disturbed soul currents cannot be set on a right course until one penetrates deeply into their origin in the unconscious.

The conscious mind wants the good and wants to act right; one part of the unconscious, the higher self, also strives upward. But in every human being another part of the personality wants what is evil and false —yet this evil or falsehood does not have to be of the criminal kind; all depends on the person's development. A more highly developed individual's negative traits weigh as heavily as the criminal tendencies of a less highly evolved being. Blind, impossible demands may rub him sore, so to speak. They cannot be fulfilled, partly because they are not realizable, and partly because they run contrary to what the higher self desires. The opposing tendencies clash and exhaust the soul, they create disharmony and sometimes illness. Above all, they prevent spiritual growth, or at least hinder maximum development. Therefore I cannot urge you enough to devote all your attention to the discovery of the unconscious: get to know the unconscious, make it conscious in meditation, in prayer, in all your striving. Without this there can be no significant progress, and you will have to experience the open and unhindered manifestation of your unconscious currents when you shed your body. Then the conflict must be entered. This will be a disappointment, for people, until they face themselves, believe that they are far more developed than they actually are, and assume that only their actions count; yet their feelings are also actions and have just as tangible consequences. Also, the development of the personality takes incomparably longer and is much more difficult to accomplish in the spirit world. God has arranged life on earth in such a way that your spiritual ascent is speeded up in the surroundings of imperfection, in the diversity of developmental stages. Yet it often happens that more incarnations are used than strictly necessary to set the imperfect, blind, unconscious currents right; some future earthly lives could be avoided by a stronger commitment to development in the present.

Let yourself be led by God entirely; open yourself to God's will alone, so that your way can be shown to you step by step. God is a generous giver, my dear ones. You will realize that when you see that what comes to you through God is more wonderful than anything you can imagine for yourself. The initial difficulty is only to entrust yourself to God. No, the question is not the giving of some material thing; this would be much easier, much more convenient. You have to give yourself. For, if you can give yourself in the right way, you can give to everyone with whom you come into contact. However, before you can give yourself, you must have gained yourself. You cannot give what you do not have.

Few people truly possess their own selves, because they do not know themselves well enough. In that state they are more or less lost to themselves. To the extent you recoil in your feelings from imperfections in yourself, to that same extent you do not possess yourself. Then you do not stand on solid ground. Almost all of you human beings are still slaves to your faults and negative feelings. Only by accepting yourselves as you are can you master these and therefore yourselves. That is how transformation and purification begins. However much outer freedom you may have, you are enslaved as long as you recoil in embarrassment from each inner imperfection and outer exposure. As slaves you cannot possess yourselves and cannot really therefore give yourselves. A consequence of this state is that you are very dependent on this or that outer happening, and thereby cannot feel harmonious. Harmony can only be created when you no longer depend on things that are beyond your control. Those who have found themselves on this most beautiful path, the path of light, no longer have to give some specific thing. Such people can give themselves totally, not only to a loved one, but also to any situation in life where God has placed them. They can give themselves with their whole soul and with their whole being.

Part Two

The Nature of God

"I don't believe in God."

"It is impossible to know if a God exists ."

"The amount of pain and injustice in the world is
so great that if there is a God, He must be a
cruel sadist."

"God is love."

"Jesus Christ is God and He has personally saved me."

Everyone has something to say about God. Some people say
they are indifferent to the idea of God. They do not hope to be
able to know if God exists, and so they choose not to dwell on
the subject. Others are passionate on the subject — either
passionately atheistic or passionately theistic and sectarian.
Those who are passionate are convinced they are right and
often feel a contempt, outspoken or veiled, for those who
believe differently.

Regardless of anyone's passion or indifference, it seems rare
that anyone changes another person's mind by argument.
However, people do change their beliefs and may in later years
passionately hold views that they passionately disavowed
before.

Those who doubt often say they cannot understand how a
God that is all-powerful and all-loving could allow so much
misery and injustice in the world. Often, such people began by
believing that the world is cruel and unjust, and they then end
in some form of atheism, thinking that they have arrived at this
conclusion by a logical path.

Others believe in God, but among the billions who do
believe there must be millions of different beliefs about the
nature of God. Even among Christians the variety of beliefs and
practices is enormous. What can be made of this confusion?
How can we understand it?

The Pathwork states that there are two main reasons for the vast differences among people in this regard. The first is that the specific images formed in childhood will determine the nature of the unconscious feelings and assumptions we will have about God as an adult. The lectures I have chosen for this section explain how people form their most basic picture of what God is. The lectures show that before we can hope to say anything of value about any subject, we must first explore the nature of our unconscious assumptions with regard to that subject.

Second, human beings evolve through stages in their relationship to God, as they go through a life, and as they go through many lives. These stages progress from, first, naïve and superstitious belief, to rational skepticism and disbelief, and finally, to a new and grounded belief which has purged itself of superstition. As human beings mature through the stages of development, their relationship to God alters dramatically.

In this section we put into words, as best as can be done with our limited human language, *what God is*, and we learn how the nature of our prayer must change, as we more clearly comprehend who we are in relationship to God.

D.T.

CHAPTER 4

The God Image
and the God THAT IS

Greetings. I bring you blessings in the Name of God. Blessed is this hour, my dearest friends.

In the Bible it is said that you should not create an image of God. Many people believe this statement means that you should not draw a picture or make a statue of God. But this is by no means the entire meaning of this statement. If you think about it a little more deeply, you will come to the conclusion that this could not be all that is implied in this commandment. You must now perceive that it refers to the inner *image*[3]. That the existence of God is so often questioned and that Divine Presence is so rarely experienced within the human soul is the result of the distorted God-image most human beings harbor.

The False Concept of God

The child experiences its first *conflict with authority* at an early age. It also learns that *God is the highest authority*. Therefore it is not surprising that the child projects its subjective experiences with authority onto its imaginings about God. Hence an image is formed; whatever the child's and later the adult's relationship to authority is, his attitude towards God will, most probably, be colored and influenced by it.

A child experiences all kinds of authority. When it is prohibited from doing what it enjoys most, it experiences authority as hostile. When parental authority indulges the child, authority will be felt as benign. When there is a predominance of one kind of authority in childhood, the reaction to that will become the unconscious attitude toward God. In many instances, however, children experience a mixture of both.

---

3. In Pathwork terminology, an **"image"** is a distorted view of reality which has hardened into a firmly held false conclusion about life. Also see the Glossary at the end of this volume.

Then the combination of these two kinds of authority will form their image of God. In the measure that a child experiences fear and frustration, to that measure will fear and frustration unconsciously be felt toward God. God is then believed to be a punishing, severe, and often even unfair and unjust force that one has to contend with. I know, my friends, that you do not think so consciously. But in this work you are used to finding the emotional reactions that do not at all correspond to your conscious concepts on whatever subject. The less the unconscious concept coincides with the conscious one, the greater is the shock when one realizes the discrepancy.

Many things the child enjoys most are forbidden. Many things that give pleasure are prohibited, usually for the child's own welfare; this the child cannot understand. It also happens that parents forbid things out of their own ignorance and fear. Thus it is impressed on the child's mind that for many things most pleasurable in the world, one is subject to punishment from God, the highest and sternest authority.

In addition, *you are bound to encounter human injustice* in the course of your life, in childhood as well as in adulthood. Particularly if these injustices are perpetrated by people who stand for authority and are therefore unconsciously associated with God, your unconscious belief in God's severe injustice is strengthened. Such experiences also intensify your fear of God.

All this forms an image which, if properly analyzed, makes a monster out of God. *This God, living in your unconscious mind, is really more of a Satan.*

You yourself have to find out in your work on yourself how much of this holds true for you personally. Is your soul impregnated with similar wrong concepts? If and when the realization of such an impression becomes conscious within a growing human being, it is often not understood that this concept of God is false. Then the person turns away from God altogether and wants no part of the monster discovered hovering in his or her mind. This, by the way, is often the true reason for someone's atheism. The turning away is just as erroneous as the opposite extreme which consists of fearing a God who is severe, unjust, self-righteous and cruel. The person who unconsciously maintains the distorted God-image rightly fears this deity and resorts to cajoling for favors. Here you have a good example of two opposite extremes, both of which lack truth to an equal extent.

Now let us examine the case in which a child experiences benign authority to a greater degree than fear and frustration with a negative authority. Let us assume the child is overindulged and pampered by doting parents who fulfill its every whim. They do not instill a sense of responsibility in the child. This causes in the personality an unconscious belief that he or she can get away with anything in the eyes of God. The child thinks it can cheat life and avoid self-responsibility. To begin with, it will know much less fear. But since life cannot be cheated, this wrong attitude will produce conflicts, and therefore fear will be generated by a chain-reaction of wrong thinking, feeling, and action. An inner confusion will arise, since life as it is in reality does not correspond to the indulgent unconscious God-image and concept.

Many subdivisions and combinations of these two main categories can exist in the same soul, and the development achieved in former incarnations in this particular respect also influences the psyche. It is very important, therefore, my friends, to find out what your God-image is. This image is basic and determines all other attitudes, images and patterns throughout your life. Do not be deceived by your conscious convictions. Rather try to examine and analyze your emotional reactions to authority, to your parents, to your fears and expectations. Out of these you will gradually discover what you *feel* about God rather than what you *think*. The whole scale between the two opposite poles of monster and doting parent is reflected in your God-image, from hopelessness and despair in the emotional conviction of an unjust universe, to self-indulgence, rejection of self-responsibility, and the expectation of a God who is supposed to pamper you.

Dissolving the God-Image

Now the question of how to dissolve such an image arises. How do you dissolve any image, that is, any wrong conclusion? First, you have to become fully conscious of the wrong concept. This must always be the first step. You may often be aware of an image — which is always false, otherwise it would not be an image — but you may not even be aware that it *is* false. In your intellectual perception you are partly convinced that the image-conclusion is correct. As long as this is so, you cannot free yourself of the enslaving chains of falsity. So the second step is to set your intellectual ideas straight. It is most important to understand that the proper formation of the intellectual concept should never be superimposed on the still lingering emotional false concept. This would only cause suppression. But, on the other hand, you should not allow the wrong conclusions and images, which rise to the surface due to the work you have done so far, make you believe that they are true. In a subtle way, this is what happens sometimes. Realize that the hitherto suppressed wrong concepts have to evolve clearly into consciousness. Formulate the right concept. Then these two should be compared. You need constantly to check how much you still deviate emotionally from the right intellectual concept.

Do this quietly, without inner haste or anger at yourself that your emotions do not follow your thinking as quickly as you would like. Give them time to grow. This is best accomplished by constant observation and comparison of the wrong and the right concept. Realize that your emotions need time to adjust, but do everything in your power to give them the opportunity to grow; it will happen by the process just stated. Observe your emotions despite the resistances and the pretexts they can muster. For there is always that part in you which resists change and growth. This part in the human personality is very shrewd. Be wise to these ruses.

The injustices in the world are so often ascribed to God, my friends. If you are convinced of the existence of injustice, the best attitude is to examine your own life and find in it how you have contributed to and even caused happenings that seemed entirely unjust. The better you understand the magnetic force of images and the powerful strength of all psychological and unconscious currents, the better will you understand and experience the truth of these teachings, and the more deeply will you be convinced that *there is no injustice*. Find the *cause and effect* of your inner and outer actions.

God Is Not Unjust

If you make half the effort you usually make when finding others' faults to find your own, you will *see the connection with your own law of cause and effect and this alone will set you free,* will show you that there is no injustice. This alone will show you that it is not God, nor the fates, nor any unjust world order wherein you have to suffer the consequences of other people's shortcomings, but your ignorance, your fear, your pride, your egotism that directly or indirectly caused that which seemed, so far, to come your way without your attracting it. Find that hidden link and you will come to see truth. You will realize that *you are not a prey to circumstances* or other people's imperfections, but really the creator of your life. Emotions are very powerful creative forces, because your unconscious affects the unconscious of the other person. This truth is perhaps most relevant to the discovery of how you call forth happenings in your life, good or bad, favorable or unfavorable.

Once you experience this, you can dissolve your God-image, whether you fear God because you believe that you live in a world of injustice and are afraid of being the prey of circumstances over which you have no control, or whether you reject self-responsibility and expect an indulgent, pampering God to lead your life for you, make decisions for you, take self-inflicted hardships from you. The realization of how you cause the effects of your life will dissolve either God-image. This is one of the main breaking-points.

This breaking-point alone will bring you the recognition that you are not a victim; that you have the power over your life; that you are free; and that these laws of God are infinitely good, wise, loving and *safe!* They do not make a puppet out of you but make you wholly free and independent.

The True Concept of God

We will try to speak about God. But remember that all words can, at best, be only a small point to start with, in cultivating your own inner recognition. Words are always insufficient; but how much more so when it concerns God who is unexplainable, who is all, who cannot be limited by words. How can your perception and your capacity to understand suffice to sense the greatness of the Creator? Every smallest inner deviation and obstruction is a hindrance to understanding. We have to be concerned with the elimination of these hindrances, step by step, stone by stone, for only then will you glimpse the light and sense the infinite bliss.

One hindrance is that despite the teachings you have received from various sources, you still unconsciously think about God as someone who acts, chooses, decides, disposes arbitrarily and at will. On top of this you superimpose the idea that all this must be just. But even though you include the notion of justice, this idea is false. For God **IS**. God's laws are made once and for all and work automatically, so to speak. Emotionally you are somehow bound to this wrong concept, and it stands in your way. As long as it is present, the real and true concept cannot fill your being.

God is, among so many other things, *life* and *life force*. Think of this life force as you think of *an electric current, endowed with supreme intelligence*. This "electric current" is there, inside you, around you, outside of yourself. It is up to you how you use it. You can use electricity for constructive purposes, even for healing; or you can use it to kill. That does not make the electric current good or bad. This power current is an important aspect of God and is one which touches you most.

This concept may raise the question whether God is personal or impersonal, directing intelligence or law and principle. Human beings, since they experience life with a dualistic consciousness, tend to believe that either the one or the other is true. Yet God is both. But God's personal aspect does not mean personality. God is not a person residing in a certain place, though it is possible to have a personal God-experience within the self. For *the only place God can be looked for and found is within,* not in any other place. God's existence can be deduced outside of the self from the beauty of Creation, from the manifestations of nature, from the wisdom collected by philosophers and scientists. But such observations become an experience of God only when God's presence is felt first within. The inner experience of God is the greatest of all experiences because it contains all desirable experiences.

The Eternal, Divine Laws

God's love is also personal in the *divine laws*, in the *being* of the laws. The love in the laws shows clearly in the fact that they are made in such a way as to lead you ultimately into light and bliss, no matter how much you deviate from them. The more you deviate from them, the more you approach them by the misery that the deviation inflicts. This misery will cause you to turn around at one point or another — some sooner, some later, but all must finally come to the point where they realize that they themselves determine their misery or bliss. This is the love in the law— this is the "Plan of Salvation."

God lets you deviate from the universal laws if you so wish. You are made in God's likeness, meaning that you are completely free to choose. You are not forced to live in bliss and light, though you can if you wish. All this expresses the love of God.

When you have difficulty in understanding the justice of the universe and the self-responsibility in your own life, do not think of God as "He" or "She." Rather think of God as the Great

Creative Power at your disposal. It is not God who is unjust; the injustice is caused by the wrong use of the powerful current at your disposal. If you start from this premise and meditate on it, and if from now on you seek to find where and how you have ignorantly abused the power current in you, God will answer you. This I can promise.

If you sincerely search for this answer and if you have the courage to face it, you will come to understand cause and effect in your life. You will understand what led you to believe (albeit until now unconsciously, hence all the more powerfully) that God's world is a world of cruelty and injustice, a world in which you have no chance, a world in which you have to be afraid and hopeless, a universe where God's Grace comes to a few chosen ones, but you are excluded. Only self responsibility can free you of this fallacy that distorts your soul and your life. This will give you confidence and the deep, absolute knowledge that you have nothing to fear.

The universe is a whole of which humanity is an organic part. To experience God is to realize oneself as an integral part of this oneness. Yet in their present inner state of development, most human beings can only experience God under the dual aspects of spontaneously active consciousness and automatic law. In actuality these two aspects form an interacting unity.

The aspect of spontaneous consciousness is the active principle, which in human terms is called the masculine aspect. It is the *life force*[4] which creates; it is potent energy. This life force permeates the entire creation and all creatures. It can be used by all conscious living beings.

The aspect of automatic law is the passive, receptive principle, the life substance or feminine aspect, which the creative principle molds, forms, and plays upon. These two aspects, together, are necessary to create anything. They are the conditions of creation and are present in every form of creation, whether it be a galaxy or a simple gadget.

When speaking of God, it is important to understand that all divine aspects are duplicated in the human being who lives and whose being rests upon the same conditions, principles, and laws as those pertaining to Cosmic Intelligence. They are both the same in essence, differentiated only by degree. Self-realization, then, means activating the maximum potential of God in oneself.

---

4. See Glossary for definition of **life force**.

God Is in You and Creates Through You

God, as deliberate, spontaneous, directing intelligence does not act *for* you but *through* you, being *in* you. It is very important that you understand this subtle but decisive difference. When you have an erroneous approach to God in this respect, you vaguely expect God to act for you. Then you resent the inevitable disappointments; hence you conclude that there is no Creator. If one could contact an outer deity, one could logically expect it to act for one. But waiting for responses outside the self means focusing into the wrong direction. When you contact God within the self, responses must come and, what is more, you will notice and understand them. Such manifestations of God's presence within the self demonstrate God's personal aspect. They demonstrate active, deliberate, directing intelligence, forever changing and fresh, adapted in infinite wisdom to any situation. They express the Spirit of God manifesting through the spirit of the human being.

When you discover yourself and, consequently, the role you play in creating your fate, you truly come into your own. You are no longer driven but are master of your life.

You must discover this by yourself. If life forced you into your true birthright in order to save you from suffering, you would never be a free creature. The very meaning of freedom implies that no force or constraint can be used, not even for good or desirable results. Not even the greatest of all discoveries on the road of your evolution would have any meaning if you were compelled to experience it. The choice to turn in the direction that will finally yield true freedom and power must be left to each individual.

Ideas, intent, thoughts, will, feelings, and attitudes as expressed by conscious beings are the greatest forces in the universe. This means that the power of spirit is superior to all other energies. If this power is understood and used according to its inherent law, it supersedes all other manifestations of power. No physical power can be as strong as the power of the spirit. Since the human being is spirit and intelligence, he or she is inherently capable of directing all automatic, blind laws. It is through this capacity that God is truly experienced.

When you deliberately contact and ask your higher self, which contains all divine aspects, for guidance and inspiration, and when you experience the result of this inner act, you will know that God is present within you.

So, my dearest friends, find out what distorted image you have of God which stands in the way of your God-experience as the total, blissful cosmic feeling it is in reality. Make yourself open to it. May the words I am giving you bring light into your soul, into your life. Let them fill your heart. Let them be an instrument to liberate you from illusions. God's world is a wonderful world and there is only reason to rejoice on whatever plane you live, whatever illusions or hardships you temporarily endure. Let them be a medicine for you, and grow strong and happy with whatever comes your way. Be blessed. Be in peace. Be in God!

CHAPTER 5

The Stages
of Relationship to God

Greetings, my dearest friends. God bless all of you. Blessed are your efforts. Blessed is your work.

Being Without Awareness

I wish to discuss your relationship to God throughout the various stages of development that all humanity undergoes. The state of being without awareness is the first stage in this great cycle. Primitive people, during their first few incarnations, are still in the state of being without awareness. They live for the moment, tending to their immediate needs. Their minds have not yet developed and are therefore not equipped to ask certain questions, to doubt, to think, to discriminate. They live in the now, but without awareness. In order to live in the now with awareness, human beings must pass through various stages of development.

As the human mind continues to develop, it will address the pressing needs that emerge in any growing civilization. In other words, the mind is first used concretely. But later it begins to be used abstractly, to ask the important questions: Where do I come from? Where do I go? What is the meaning of life? What is the significance of this universe?

People begin to perceive nature and its laws. They observe the magnificence of natural law, and they begin to wonder. This wonder represents the first conscious step toward relating to the Creator.

Who created these laws? Who made all this? Is any superior mind responsible for this creation? With such questions, the first concepts of God come into existence. Thus, when people conclude that there must be someone of such infinite superiority, wisdom and intelligence, they feel they must relate to this Supreme Being.

But simultaneously, humanity's spiritual and emotional immaturity produces fear and many other problematic emotions, coloring the concept of a superior Creator. On the one hand, people want an authority who thinks for them, who decides for them and is thus responsible for them. They cling to this authority, hoping to be relieved of self-responsibility. On the other hand, they project onto this God their fears of life and of their inadequacy to cope with it. They sense the power of this immensely wise and resourceful Creator of all the natural laws. Since they cannot yet separate power from cruelty, they begin to fear this God, created from their own projections. Thus they begin to appease, cajole, submit to and become subdued by this imaginary God-image.

To recapitulate: The first state of awakening causes people to wonder. In this spontaneous experience of wonder, they often have a genuine God-experience and relationship. But then, as they grow more conflicted and fearful and their desires become more urgent, all these emotions and attitudes color the first God-experience and they no longer relate genuinely, spontaneously or creatively to God, but rather submit to a projection of themselves.

The more the mind grows in only one direction, unaccustomed to resolving its unconscious conflicts, the falser the relationship to God becomes. The relationship is false because it is based on personal needs, on wishful thinking and on fear. The longer the distortion continues, the falser the concept of God becomes — consciously or unconsciously. In the end, it will become a superstition, with less and less truth and more dogma, making a farce of God.

Eventually their intelligence, which has grown in the meantime, will prevent people from continuing this way indefinitely. Their intelligence will tell them, "There cannot possibly be a Father who leads our life for us. Life is up to us; it is our responsibility. We have free will." At that point, a reaction sets in, and people often turn to the other extreme and become atheists.

The Stage of Atheism

Atheism exists in two states: (1) as an absolute lack of awareness and understanding of life and the laws of nature; (2) as a reaction to the superstitious God-image and self-projection of humanity, which comes from denying self-responsibility. This latter state, erroneous as it is, is still a higher state of development than the original belief in God, which grew predominantly from fear, evasion, escapism, wishful thinking and denial of self-responsibility. The latter is often a necessary transition on the way to a more realistic and genuine experience of and relationship to God. During this stage, human faculties are cultivated that are of utmost importance for individual growth.

This does not mean that I advocate atheism any more than I advocate a childish, clinging belief in God. Both are stages. In each stage the soul learns something important that lasts long after the superficial layers of the mind have dispensed with both false extremes.

In the second state of atheism, people learn to assume self-responsibility. They let go of the wished-for hand that leads life for them and absolves them from the consequences of their own mistakes. Atheism makes people give up the expectation of being rewarded for their obedience to rules. Simultaneously, it frees them from the fear of punishment. In some ways, it brings people back to themselves.

Growing Beyond Atheism

But when a certain point is passed in this stage it is no longer possible to remain an atheist. Once any scientific fact or philosophy is carried to its logical conclusion, it is no longer possible to maintain an untruth or half-truth — or even a temporary state that once served a healthy function. When people pass through these various stages, they are bound to arrive at the point where they use their minds to question their own motives and begin to look into themselves.

People cultivate awareness by facing the reality within. As they proceed, ever deeper levels of the psyche become liberated. The outcome of this liberation is inevitably a genuine God-experience, which is very different from the childish belief in a self-projected God that the mind has created out of fear, weakness and wishful thinking. You no longer act according to what you feel God demands or expects. You live in the now. You do not fear your own imperfection nor God's punishing you for it. You can see the imperfection without becoming frantic.

Once people understand imperfection without fearing it, they will see that it is not the imperfection itself that is so harmful, but their lack of awareness of it, the fear of being punished for it, the pride of wanting to be above it. Once they stop feeling frantic about overcoming it, they will feel calm enough to observe it and understand why it exists. In this very process, they outgrow it. As people cultivate this attitude, they are genuinely able to experience God. Also, the occasional glimpse of imperfection does promote the proper attitude toward oneself.

The genuine God-experience is one of *being*. God is not perceived as acting— doling out punishments or rewards, or guiding you in a specific way so that you can avoid human effort. You simply realize that God *is*. This experience is very difficult to explain in words, my friends, but it is the only way I can say it. You cannot come to the feeling that God *is* if you do not first face what is in you right now, however imperfect, faulty or childish it may be.

It would be misleading to assume that each of the stages I have roughly described here follow neatly one after the other. They overlap. They do not always follow in this order, because the human personality is made up of more than one level, which as you know, conflict. Different layers of the personality express different attitudes at any given time. Hence, it is possible that at one period of your life you may be consciously in one stage, unconsciously in another. Only after you proceed on a path of self-knowledge such as this, does the unconscious stage come to the fore. That is why in a later stage something often comes out that seems to belong in an earlier stage. This also happens when a certain necessary stage was not fully lived through but repressed due to outer influences and pressures. So my description is only a general outline. Beware of judging yourself or another according to what you see.

Being in Awareness

Self-awareness must eventually lead to the more general state of *being in awareness*. Simultaneously, a new relationship to God comes into existence. God is now experienced as *being*. I repeat, you cannot enter this stage if you do not first experience the negative aspects of your current reality. Nor can you come to it by learning concepts, observing philosophies and practices or following doctrines. If you are unwilling to experience and be in your present confusions, errors and pains, by facing and understanding them, you cannot ever *be* in God. Or, to put it in other words, you cannot be in a state of happiness, peace or creativity, without strife, if you do not face the temporary, often unpleasant reality. Only then can the greater reality be experienced. At first it will come occasionally in vague glimpses, but even this will give you a new approach and relationship to God. It will not only transform your attitude and concept of God, but also your concepts about yourself and your place in life.

Needless to say, in your relationship to God, your prayer — meaning your speaking to God — also expresses the various phases. It is often the case, as it is with all things on earth, that you are actually inwardly already in a new stage, while outwardly you still cling to old habits. This may apply not only to the way you pray, but also to certain concepts you cling to. The mind is intrinsically habit-forming, but experiencing *being* never forms habits. The memory and the mind's tendency to form habits are a source of danger to true spiritual experience. The more flexible you are, the less likely you will fall into the trap of habit, of clinging to old ideas that once gave you an experience that you wish to recreate by holding on to it.

If you steadily train yourself to face what is in you now, you free yourself of habits that hold you back from productive living, from true experience, whether this is God, life, yourself— it is all the same. It is being. Is it not habit that ingrained certain experiences so deeply in your mind that they turned into rigid images? Is it not habit that causes you to stick to misconceptions, generalizations that are always half-truths at best? This applies to many things, my friends.

Again, I wish to emphasize that whenever you discover such erroneous ways in yourself, beware of feeling guilty, of growing frantic, of feeling "I should not." This attitude is the greatest barrier of all!

Free Will and Predestination

And now, my friends, let us turn to your questions.

QUESTION: I tried to explain what you told us about the spirit and free will to two people —one very religious, and the other a scientist. They then asked, "If God is omniscient and loving, does He then also know the future? If He knows the future, while He gave us free will, He must know what we will do with it." And this I cannot answer.

ANSWER: In the first place, the future is a product of time. And time is a product of the mind. Therefore, in reality, the future does not exist, just as the past does not exist. I realize that this is impossible for most people to understand. Outside the mind, there is being —that is, no past, present or future, only now. This can, at best, be vaguely sensed by feeling, rather than intellect.

Furthermore, this question arises from the same total misconception I outlined in this very lecture in that it shows the concept of a God who acts, does. Creation is, in the true sense, not an action, and certainly not a time-bound action. When God created spirit, it was out of time, out of mind, in the state of being. Each spirit is, in this sense, God-like and creates its own life. God does not take away or add on.

Moreover, I have this to add: It is a complete illusion to believe that pain and suffering are terrible in themselves. Please, try to understand what I am saying. Humanity's inordinate fear of suffering is utterly unrealistic and, again, an erroneous product of the mind. People fear pain and suffering mainly because they believe they have nothing to do with it, that it can come without their being responsible for it — in other words, that it is either an injustice or chaotic coincidence.

Actual suffering is not half as frightening as the fear of it. To a slight degree, many of you have experienced this. You have experienced that when you fear something before it happens, it seems so much worse than when you actually go through it. And you have also come to recognize how you have created such events. If you observe this chain of events within, abstaining from perfectionism, moralizing and justifying, the pain instantly recedes, even though the outer situation may remain the same. When you truly come to terms with your reality, you can also accept the imperfection of life. When you stop rebelling against imperfection, many patterns change, and you cause less suffering for yourself. But your conscious or unconscious expectation that life should be perfect makes you rebel and erect barriers that cause more imperfection and suffering than life would otherwise bring.

So it is your attitude toward suffering, toward life and toward yourself that determines how you experience suffering. If your attitude toward suffering were less distorted than it usually is, you would find that the problems you have to solve in conquering mind and matter are beautiful. They are the most beautiful things in your earth life. Only by conquering your own resistance and blindness, your lack of awareness of yourself, will you experience the beauty of life, even though you sometimes go through difficult periods.

When people come closer to understanding this, questions about free will and determinism can never be asked. The question is so confused, contains so much blindness and lack of awareness of reality, it shows such spiritual immaturity that it cannot even be answered in any way that will make sense to the questioner. You cannot understand with the mind what is beyond the realm of the mind. For that, another faculty is necessary, but as long as the existence of such a faculty is denied, how can you even lead the person to an eventual understanding?

This question also contains an eternal conflict between religious concepts. On the one hand, it postulates that God is an omnipotent Father who acts at will, who rewards you if you obey his laws, who guides you without your active participation in your own inner life, provided you humbly ask Him to. On the other hand, it postulates that humans have free will, that they mold their own fate, that they are responsible for their lives. While religion teaches the latter, it simultaneously cripples free decision and self-responsibility by forcing people to obey certain prescribed rules. People are confused by these two apparently mutually exclusive concepts. The question you asked typifies such confusion.

An omnipotent Creator and human self-responsibility are mutually exclusive only when viewed in time through the mind and when this omnipotent Creator is perceived as acting like a human being. You do not yet have to have reached the state of awareness to sense that, in reality, there is no conflict between the two. All you have to do is face yourself without resistance, without the pretense of being more than you are, without striving to be more perfect than you happen to be at this moment. Each individual aspect that you view in yourself with such freedom puts you at that moment into a state of being, and you inwardly perceive the truth of God as being without contradictions of the sort you asked in your question. Then you will know, profoundly, that complete self-responsibility is not exclusive to a Supreme Being. A person who is inwardly not ready cannot possibly understand what I am saying here.

The Stages of Prayer

QUESTION: Will you please elaborate on the meaning of prayer in the different stages?

ANSWER: Prayer will be adapted to the conscious concepts

of any given phase. In the very first stage, when people are still in the stage of being without awareness, there is no prayer, because there is no God concept. In the next stage, when people begin to ask questions, this wondering serves as prayer or meditation. The next stage may be the realization of a supreme intelligence. In this stage, prayer takes the form of admiration of the marvel of the universe and nature. It is worship. In the next stage, when confusion, coupled with immaturity and inadequacy, causes fear, helplessness and dependency, prayer will take the form of supplication, wishful thinking, and denial of reality. When prayers seem to be answered in this state, it is not because God acts, but because, in some way, people are sincere despite all their self-deceptions and evasions and have thus opened a channel through which the power of the laws of being can penetrate. This is an important distinction that will be perceived only at a later stage.

When people realize their own participation in having a prayer answered, they will lose the sense of helplessness before an arbitrary willful God whom they have to appease by man-made, superimposed rules. But I might also add that what appears to be an answered prayer is often actually the result of having resolved inner conflicts, at least for the time being.

When people enter the stage of independence and let go of their imaginary God who punishes, rewards and leads their life for them, they find themselves in the stage of atheism, of denial of any higher being, and they do not pray, of course — at least not in the conventional sense. They may meditate; they may look at themselves sincerely, and this, as you all know by now, is prayer in the true sense. But people in the atheistic stage may also be completely irresponsible and fail to think and look at themselves. They may escape from themselves just as the person who uses God as an escape does.

When people reach the stage of active self-awareness, of facing themselves as they really are, they may, at first, still be accustomed to the old prayer of begging for help, asking God to do for them what they shy away from doing themselves. Yet, despite this habit, they begin to face themselves. Only after reaching deeper levels of such self-facing will people gradually avoid the kind of prayer they were used to. They may even go through a stage of not actively praying at all, in the usual sense. But they meditate — and that is often the best prayer! They meditate by looking at their real motivations, by allowing their actual feelings to come to the surface and questioning them. In this kind of activity, prayer in the old sense becomes more and more meaningless and contradictory. Prayer is, in fact, the act of self-awareness and of looking at oneself in truth. Prayer is the sincere intent to face what may be most unpleasant. This is prayer because it contains the attitude that truth for its own sake is the threshold to love. Without truth and without love there can be no God-experience. Love cannot grow out of trying to pretend a truth that is not felt. But love can grow out of facing a truth, no matter how imperfect it is. This attitude is prayer. Candor with oneself is prayer; alertness to one's resistance is prayer; owning up to something that one has hidden from in shame is prayer. When this happens, the state of being gradually emerges, though perhaps with interruptions. Then, *in the state of being, prayer is no longer an act of uttering words or thoughts. It is a feeling of being in the eternal now;* of flowing in a current of love with all beings; of understanding and perception; of being alive.

These comprise prayer in the highest sense. Prayer is awareness of God in His reality. But this kind of prayer cannot be imitated or learned through any teachings, prescribed practices or disciplines. It is the natural outcome of the courage and humility to face oneself completely and without reservation. Before you have reached this highest state of relating to God, a state of being where prayer and being are one, all you can do is to practice the best prayer in the world by constantly renewing the intent to face yourself without any reservation, to remove all pretenses between what you want to be and what you truly are, and then remove the pretense between yourself and others. This is the way of the path, my friends.

With this, I bless each and every one of you. Try to feel the love, the warmth and the truth that comes from the world of being, which can be yours for the asking. You have a key now. Use it! Be in peace, be in God!

Part Three

The Great Transition from Self-Centeredness to Love

"God does not ask anything else of you
except that you let yourself go
and let God be God in you."

—*Meister Eckhart*

The Pathwork provides a powerful metaphor for our work when it speaks of the "great transition." On one side of the great transition is our work to become relaxed, fulfilled, free human beings. On the other side is our releasing all this to simply align with the will of God.

Of course our lifetime of self-work will not precisely reflect such a conclusive transition from one state to the other. Deep in our souls we've always had places that are fearlessly aligned with God's will. And we may have nagging personal issues that will require us to keep examining and working on them all our lives. The Pathwork lectures reflect this interwoven, cyclical nature of the work, alternating between very basic instructions in dealing with troublesome personality issues, while also beckoning us toward total surrender to the Divine. The overarching spirit of the lectures, however, never deviates from the premise that our final aim is far greater than mere self-improvement.

The first chapter of the first Pathwork book, *The Pathwork of Self-Transformation*, offers a useful contrast between this work and mainstream psychotherapy: "It is essential to deal with confusions, inner misconceptions, destructive attitudes, alienating defenses, negative emotions, and paralyzed feelings, all of which psychotherapy also attempts to do and even posits as its ultimate goal. In contrast, the Pathwork enters its most important phase only after this first stage is over. The second and most important phase consists of learning how to activate the greater consciousness dwelling within every human soul." *(From Pathwork Lecture #204)*

What is this "greater consciousness dwelling within every human soul"? It is the capacity to love, to be "in" love, in God. The Pathwork stresses that love is not something that we can command ourselves to feel, or that we can intellectually decide to feel. Love is not even really a feeling. It is a state of being, of surrender, of perfect faith, that transcends and can empower all feelings. Love is giving up any sense of separation, from any part of oneself, from other human beings, from the natural world, and from the spiritual realms. Love is eternal and also being born every moment. At bottom, all true spiritual instructions are aimed at helping us step into this eternal moment of love.

Before the great transition, I still believe that I am improving myself. I am involved in personal growth. I am self-actualizing. I am finding and expressing all of my feelings. I am reclaiming my body. I am expanding to my fullest human potential.

I am re-owning parts of myself that I earlier had learned to disown. In this sense I am in the process of getting "bigger."

When I truly make the great transition, I feel the rug being pulled out from under my carefully constructed self-actualized self. I lose the sense that I am "growing." Instead, for a time, I may feel like I am losing myself. Instead of continuing to get bigger, I feel myself getting smaller, even insignificant, as my personal goals for myself fade and seem to become irrelevant.

The transition can be described as a movement from self-centered isolation to a state of union. But this is not the "union" that I fantasize while I still am living in separateness. While I am living in my state of believing that I am a separate me, I can think I have some sense of what being in union means. I can even perhaps convince myself at times that I have arrived at that state. But then some experience disabuses me of this notion, and I am back in what is clearly a separate and self-centered existence.

Paradoxically, however, when I humbly allow myself to become small, I make the transition to becoming "bigger" again, but from a whole new perspective. The old "big" came to me through reincorporating blocked aspects of myself, building positive beliefs and habits to replace my old, limiting ones, and all the other work of strengthening and improving the self. On the contrary, I now become bigger by thinning my boundaries, by offering myself up to the infinite flow of spiritual energies within and around me, by totally surrendering any sense that I am in charge or that I know what God's plan is for me or for the world.

In Pathwork terms, one noticeable feature of work at this level is that it no longer involves the mask. The mask is a creation of the personality, and by this point in our journey we will have substantially worked through the personality issues that created and maintained our idealized, mask self.

The effect is to expose in stark clarity the conflict between the lower self and the higher self at the soul level. As we have experienced all along, the lower self is invested in separation and fear, the higher self in love and truth. Now, at the level of the soul, this split becomes much clearer. The lower self's commitment to negativity and duality now attaches to destructive forces much greater than anything that exists in our mere personalities. It is here that we must confront negative archetypes, demonic impulses, deep distortions in basic masculine and feminine energies—true evil.

Here also, however, the higher self reveals its true power, with its infinite commitment to unity, to grace, to creation. We experience our higher self as deeply trustworthy as it brings forth personal soul gifts, fosters a fertile balance of masculine and feminine, and enlists the aid of angelic impulses and spirit guides. The ultimate expression of the higher self is Christ — not as a historical figure or religious symbol, but as the fundamental helping, healing force available to us as a gift from God. As we increasingly surrender to God, as individuals and as a species, the collective lower self that we all have a part in generating will heal and come home to the love and joy at the center of creation.

Again, this great transition does not happen just once for me. Or rather, it may need to happen just once on the spiritual level; but it can take a lifetime of work to align my physical, mental and emotional self to this threshold that I have already joyfully crossed in my soul.

At the start it may seem as though **the boundaries of all and everything have loosened** up a bit. My wife and I discover that, even though we have not been speaking to each other for an hour or more, we are each having the same thought at the same time. The pain I feel for the suffering of others in the world goes beyond a commonplace empathy, and it seems to me that I am truly feeling the pain of others as keenly as though it were my own. I sense more and more that the feelings I have are not truly *my* feelings at all; and instead I experience how I am simply tuning into a certain band on the emotional radio which is possessed by all human beings. Or, stranger still, I may suddenly catch a glimpse of an angelic being standing beside me.

These of course are only beginning indications. They do not necessarily mean that I have made the great transition, but they do indicate that I am moving steadily in that direction. And if I react to such events with calmness and faith, I can better learn how to continue the process of loosening my boundaries and realizing that I am now working not primarily for myself but instead for all beings. I can further dedicate the space of my heart to the love of God, within me and flowing through me, in faith that I can be simultaneously big enough and small enough to let this love guide my destiny and that of the planet.

The next three chapters describe this great transition from self-centeredness to all-centeredness, or God-centeredness. To cross over this divide, to make the move from self-work to God-work, is the most essential step on the spiritual path of each and every being.

D.T.

CHAPTER 6

The Great Transition
in Human Development

Greetings, my dearest friends. Blessings for all of you. Blessed is this hour.

From Isolation to Union

There are two basic currents in the universe. One is the love-force, which gives of itself, communicates, and rises above the little self. In truth, the little ego which considers itself the center of all things is actually only a part of a stupendous whole. Your real self never considers you as the ultimate end. When you reach the height of your capabilities, you no longer experience life within the confines of your restricting, separating barriers of false beliefs and misconceptions. Then you find union with all people. You feel, experience, and think in an entirely different way. You become a different person, while yet remaining essentially the same individual.

The second basic force is the inverted, egocentric principle by which most human beings still live. In that state you suffer and "enjoy" life alone. No matter how many dear ones may be around you, loving and sharing with you, your life's experience is essentially unique and peculiarly your own, unsharable and untransmittable. You are the only one who experiences this particular pain or joy in quite this way. You may not ever think so consciously. In fact, your outer knowledge may contradict this inner state of experiencing life. Yet when it comes to your real feelings, this is how you experience life as long as you are still in the state of self-centered separateness.

The transition from self-centered isolation to the state of union with all is the most essential step on the evolutionary path of an individual spirit entity. At some time, in one life or another, *the transition has to come.* Exactly when this will occur varies with each individual. But on this path the time must come, sooner or later, and let us hope it comes while you are still in this particular incarnation, when you will swing over from one state to the other.

Words will not convey to you what this change really means. You have heard them many times from many philosophies and teachings. You may even be capable of discussing the subject quite intelligently. In isolated moments you may even have experienced what I am describing. But then the experience vanishes, and you are back in the old state of isolation. It takes a lot more work to make the transition permanent, and the most essential prerequisite for permanence is the finding and solving of your hidden conflicts.

Moreover, it is of vital importance that you understand that the ultimate aim of your spiritual path is to make the transition from one state into another. In order to do so, you must become fully aware that you still live in the old, undesirable state. As long as you have illusions about that, or as long as you are confused and do not even know that there are two distinctly different states, you will have a much harder time.

When you first glimpse the new state of being, you will experience a liberation from the confining wall of isolating self-centeredness. You will feel a deep purpose in life, your life, all life! You will understand the purpose of all your experiences, both the good and the bad, and will evaluate them from a completely new point of view. You will deeply experience union with all beings and the importance of their purpose as well as your own. A new joy and security will penetrate you such as you have never known. The new security will not be accompanied by the delusion that no more suffering will come to you, but you will not cringe from such suffering. You will know that it cannot harm you.

You Don't Produce Your Feelings

A common first experience in the new state is the feeling that whatever you experience at the moment is also felt by millions of other people. It was felt by millions in the past and will be felt by millions in the future. Ever since the world of matter began, all these feelings —good or bad, positive or negative, joyful or painful—have existed and people have experienced them. That you seem to produce a feeling does not mean that you have actually done so. What you do produce is the condition of tuning into the particular force or principle of an already existing emotion. This distinction may appear like hairsplitting, but it is not. To perceive life from the new outlook is an essentially different experience. As long as you harbor the illusion that you are producing the respective emotion or life-experience, you are still unique, alone, and separate. When you begin to feel that you are tuning into what already exists, you automatically become a part of the whole and can no longer be the separate individual you have felt yourself to be.

I do not expect that these words will immediately produce this new state in you. But your work on the path progresses steadily, and if you train your inner perception by meditating and trying to feel these words, you may accelerate the transition. Recognizing your commonality with all others will widen your horizon considerably; it will give you a new outlook on your passing sorrows, and it will help you to make constructive use of any negative finding within yourself. It will also heighten your creative abilities.

Humanity's fundamental longing is to actually participate in the new state of being that follows the transition. You may obstruct it and fear it in your ignorance, but the longing always remains. For in the state that is natural for all of God's creatures— the state of union— there is no aloneness any more. In your present state, you are still essentially alone. The best you can occasionally achieve is the realization that others go through similar experiences and feel the same way. But that is not at all what the new state really is.

In the new state you will know deeply that all things, feelings, emotions, thoughts and experiences already exist and that you share in any of the existing currents because of self-produced conditions. These forces and principles work all around and within you. It is up to you which one will affect you.

Visualize all emotional experiences, from the lowest to the highest, as streams or currents. According to your personal frame of mind, state of emotion, general development, character tendencies, as well as passing moods or outer happenings, you tune into one of these currents, while you may simultaneously be partly tuned into another, conflicting one. With this approach, a drastic change is bound to occur in your entire inner and outer outlook. From a separate, self-centered being you are bound to become, little by little, the being you actually are.

You imagine with your limited thinking capacity that only as a unique individual do you have dignity and a chance for happiness. You also feel —often unconsciously— that if you are but a cog in a wheel, you do not count. You are still under the illusion that you are but one out of billions, and therefore your happiness is not important. Another illusion misinterprets the right to individuality; it claims that you are a separate being and therefore essentially detached, alone and unique. At best, you believe that others may be in a similar plight. This is an illusion, but it does exist in most of you in some measure. As long as this misunderstanding is within you, you are unconsciously fighting an unnecessary and tragic battle. You think you have to be opposed to giving up your individual right to be happy and important. If this inner error — that you are fighting for your individuality and happiness when in fact you struggle to preserve your separateness — were cleared up, it would make the fight easier.

Leaving Separateness

The truth — and you will experience it one day — is this: In the new state you will see that being no more and no less than a part of a whole and sharing with so many others something that already exists, makes you a happier person. You have the right to happiness and you have more rather than less dignity and individuality because of this fact. Your dignity will increase to the extent that your pride of separateness decreases. The fullness and richness of life will increase to the extent that you leave your state of separateness in which you assume that in order to have more for yourself you have to take away from others. That is the error and the conflict. In the old state, that is the way it works out. In the new state this is not true. The importance of your welfare is infinitely greater just because you are a part of a whole. The moment you gain even a momentary glimpse of the truth, you will never again be torn by the old conflict that either you can have a happiness that is selfish, or, if you choose to refrain from this "selfishness," your happiness is unimportant.

This inherent misunderstanding causes a deep guilt in the human soul because you don't know what to do with your desire to be happy. The conflict will vanish the moment you train your outlook to take in the new approach. The instant you have experienced that first glimmer of understanding you will recognize how steeped in separateness you were. The moment the insight comes you will truly see that the old state of separateness was, and still is, your world. Then your conscious desire to leave the old world behind will increase.

When I say self-centeredness I do not use the word in a moralizing, blaming, admonishing way, but philosophically. It indicates one basic state of being as opposed to an entirely different state of being; one world, or one soul principle, as against another.

As you gradually make this transition, your values are bound to change. Your purpose, your aim, and your concept of life are bound to change. This change will not be the superficial adoption of new opinions, but a very natural, gradual, organic, inner growth. The change comes slowly; it is an inner change rather than an outer. It happens often that your outer opinions do not even have to undergo a drastic revision. They may essentially remain the same, but you will experience and feel them differently.

People are so afraid of change. But you have nothing to fear. Much of your life and your opinions may remain the same while you change. This sounds like a paradox, my friends, but it is not. To remain the same and yet to change is possible in a good, constructive, and natural way because the call of your life is to grow to the maximum. However, it is also possible to change and remain the same in some wrong and destructive ways.

Truly, you have nothing to fear in approaching this great transition, for that which is valuable and valid, that which is essentially you, will remain the same, only enriched. Only that which was not essentially you will gradually fall off, like an old outworn cloak. Creative forces of which you are still completely unaware will flow out of you.

The direction of your innermost currents will be reversed when you attain the new state of oneness. In your present state of isolation, many creative forces, such as love or talents, try to stream out of you, but due to your basic inner state of self-centered separateness they are turned back. After the initial effort of streaming out, reaching the cosmos, and teaching others, they are withdrawn, held back, and made inactive. Your innermost nature rebels against such great frustration because it is against nature, against creation, and against harmony.

This basic rebellion of your inner nature causes many conflicts that can never be solved entirely by recognizing your images and conflicts, which were created through childhood conditions. While the dissolution of childhood conflicts is essential in order to bring about the new state of being, it is important to recognize that dissolving childhood conflicts is not an end in itself. If your aim is to stop short at resolving childhood conflicts and straightening out psychological deviations, you are bound to fail in fulfilling yourself. In many instances you will not even succeed in really resolving these conflicts, if their resolution is not a means toward the greater aim: the transition from the self-centered state of isolation into the state of union with all. This includes the recognition of yourself as an integral part of Creation which strives endlessly and ceaselessly toward a greater fulfillment.

Only when you take the greater aim of union with all as your personal goal will you be capable of utterly fulfilling yourself. You will develop all your capacities, and then the great stream of life, of health, and of strength will flow through you. When your ultimate outlook on life is distorted or not clearly formulated, your creative and health-giving forces cannot be regenerated by the great cosmic stream. The cosmic forces are constantly blocked and halted by your ignorance, confusion, lack of awareness, or the wrong perspective on the real meaning of life. With the proper outlook, you are bound to approach and finally make the transition.

In the new state, your own creative forces will flow out of you naturally, allowing the cosmic forces to constantly flow into you, renewing and regenerating your entire being. Your outgoing forces will touch other beings who are attuned to them, wherever and whoever they are.

I know that this topic is difficult to understand. It is abstract and not easily put into practice. It needs all your inner senses, your intuitive nature, as well as your sincere desire to really understand the deeper meaning of these words. Through study and meditation, through trying to feel and use your own inner findings with the help of this overview, you will come to the point where these words will be a revelation to you. Then a new door will open through which you will enter gladly. You will then recognize how long you have battled to step across this threshold.

The cultivation of this new approach to life will eventually reveal to you an understanding not only of yourself and others, but also about your purpose in the universe and your function in it. Nothing else can give you the real security you are still searching for.

All great teachers and sages have spoken, in various ways, about this great transition. You who are on this path should think about it, envision it, and know that its time is bound to come.

How the human soul struggles against this, the ultimate fate of every being! How afraid it is to leave a state of unhappiness for a state of happiness and security! How foolish of you to fear, deep within your hearts, that in leaving the old world and attaining the new you have to leave something precious behind. Try to find that unreasonable, irrational fear and resistance. It is right there in you. All you have to do is look at it. You do not have to reach very far or deep to find the fear. The basic resistance to transition is expressed in innumerable little ways in your everyday life. Find it, and you will have found a valuable key. First it is necessary that you become aware of how you are struggling to maintain the isolated life, in which, at best, you want to share your life with a few chosen individuals. If you can give some manner of love to those few, you are already a step beyond many who cannot even do this.

I hope my words will not be misunderstood to mean that you should undertake a drastic change in your outer life. The transition is much more subtle than that. Once you begin to recognize the symptoms of your old, self-centered, isolated way of life, you are bound to see how every impulse related to this outlook creates fear and insecurity and is futile and senseless. The new state is one of continuous joy and deep inner security. I do not mean that difficulties cannot come your way any more. I have said that many times before and I do not ever want to be misunderstood on that subject. No one should contemplate this path and the development taking place on it with the idea that if you proceed properly your difficulties will cease. That expectation is, of course, utterly unrealistic and wrong as long as you are incarnated as a human being. However — as I said before — that which you need to go through will not frighten you anymore. It will make sense to you, and you will go through it courageously, growing with and from it. You will accept it as part of life, instead of shrinking away from it.

So you see, my dear friends, what humanity is actually struggling to maintain is a state of isolating darkness. It is a senseless struggle from which you reap unhappiness, and this alone proves that the direction is wrong and must be changed. The results of changing your inner direction are freedom and joy, purpose and security. It appears as though you were giving up something that you are actually holding on to frantically, but once you decide to let it go you will see that you have given up nothing.

The first tentative steps in the transition from one state or world into another are self-knowledge and the understanding of your unconscious problems, concepts, and attitudes. Self-knowledge and self-acceptance are the prerequisites. Everything else arises from that. You also have to realize that there is a further goal beyond the mere dissolution of your inner problems. Or, to put it differently, you cannot truly solve these problems unless you envisage this great basic transition.

If you can occasionally feel what I have tried to convey to you in this lecture, it may help you to open a little window from which you can glean a new perception. I leave you with strength and our love, and with our wishes that you may continue to struggle on this one path, this path of finding yourselves and developing yourselves to become the person you are meant to be. For there is nothing more worthwhile and purposeful that you could possibly do, as long as you are truly honest with yourself. Self-honesty is the first step toward love. So be blessed, my dearest ones, be in peace, be in God!

CHAPTER 7

The Process of Growing from Duality to Unity

Greetings, my dearest friends. I usually start these lectures by giving a blessing. Now what does the word "blessing" mean? Let us consider its deepest meaning.

"Blessing" means the vigorous total wish for good, coming from the innermost self, from the divine inner being. When this unobstructed wish flows directly into the deepest regions of consciousness of another person, a vibrating energy force is created that affects that person's consciousness.

Whenever you hear the word "blessing" from now on, it will be very helpful for you to remember that your response is necessary to make the blessing effective. Openness, willingness, and complete inner cooperation are necessary to enable two forces to meet, for a one-sided blessing is no blessing.

Our topic now is the process of growing, as it relates to *unity and duality*[5]. There are two basic ways to approach life and the self. Or, to put it differently, there are two fundamental possibilities for human consciousness: the dualistic and the unified plane. Human consciousness, perception, and experience are generally geared to the dualistic principle. This means that everything is perceived in opposites — good or bad, desirable or undesirable, life or death. As long as humanity lives in this dualism, conflict and unhappiness must persist. Absolute, universal, cosmic truth is always unified and transcends opposites in the realization that the belief in opposites is illusion.

Unification does not mean, however, that the *good* of the dualistic "either/or" is realized. People who believe this misconception follow an erroneous path: They hope to attain one of the illusory opposites as the "salvation." As long as one opposes one side and clings to the other, self-realization or liberation— that is, the unitive principle — is unattainable.

---

5. See Glossary for definition of **Unity and Duality**.

The good of the unitive principle is of an entirely different nature than the good of dualism. The former conciliates both sides, while the latter separates them. This can be ascertained in any individual problem once it is thoroughly understood. This point is extremely important to understand, my friends. For when you seek one side of a pair of opposites, you must oppose the other side. In that opposition your soul is agitated and fearful, and in that state you can never attain unity.

Dualistic Consciousness and Growth

Let us apply this distinction to the growth process. As long as human consciousness is geared to duality and cannot transcend it, the growth process is very problematic. Growth is movement in time and space; therefore, *growth on the dualistic plane automatically moves from one extreme toward its opposite.* From the moment you are born you move toward death. From the moment you unfold and grow toward fulfillment, the downward curve of destruction begins. From the moment you strive for any kind of happiness, you must fear its opposite. In ever-changing rhythm, the cyclic, eternal movement of growth must inevitably approach its opposite. It moves from life to death to life and back; from construction to destruction to construction. One brings forth the other.

It is exceedingly important to understand this concept, for it is one of the major reasons you resist growth. This belief causes a deep resistance, beyond the psychological quirks of neurosis. This fundamental opposition to growth is still found even after neuroses have been transcended and dissolved. This explains why, as long as you perceive life in dualistic terms, you fear growth; for you fear that reaching a goal will bring on its destruction. You delude yourself by fighting against time, by "postponing" fulfillment and thus also the feared opposite. The status quo, stagnation, creates agitation, or movement in the distorted sense.

As long as growth takes place on the dualistic plane, there is always a peak to be reached, and after that peak, a descent. And so all living things on the dualistic plane move in a perpetual cycle of life and death, construction and destruction, of being and becoming. In nature, the plant grows in spring toward fruition in summer. In the fall it slowly dies. In the winter it is no more. Only its dormant life potential slumbers in the soil, waiting for the seed to grow again in spring. This is the growth process. The joy during the upward curve can never be full and carefree, without anxiety, for even before the peak is reached, the downside will be anticipated.

The Unified Plane

On the unified plane of consciousness, because there are no more opposites to be feared, the dichotomy no longer exists. Self-realization always leads to the experience and perception of the unitive state. Conversely, the unitive state cannot come about any other way than through self-realization.

Self-realization means shedding the layers of error so that the real self, the divine, eternal inner being, comes to the fore. You can shed these layers of pain, error, confusion, and limitation only when you no longer run away from yourself; when you are willing to look at yourself as you really are instead of as you want to be; when you accept yourself in the moment, when you do not struggle against your temporary state, even though you understand its error. This is the work you are doing on this path.

It is entirely erroneous to assume that unitive perception cannot occur on the earthly plane. It *is* possible, absolutely possible, for anyone willing to expand his or her consciousness. Expansion is a very simple process of questioning the verity of your limited ideas, the correctness of what you assume to be unalterably thus and so. This, in turn, can be done only when you honestly look at your most subtle moods and reactions and translate them into concise words. You then find out that these reactions and reflexes, these emotions and moods, are based on certain assumptions you have never questioned, since all is kept in the dark of vagueness and easy rationalization.

This is why your pathwork is of such immeasurable importance; for without recognizing the daily little dishonesties, self-deceptions, and erroneous assumptions, you cannot question them and loosen them to make room for a new reality. Whenever a vague disturbance is honestly examined and verbalized, the concept on which the disturbance is based can be revealed and questioned. This step widens your perception, enabling you to transcend your dualism and perceive the unitive state. This has to be done in every area of consciousness, in every facet of your existence, for it is possible to realize the unitive principle in some areas, while other areas are still deeply submerged in the illusion and pain of dualism. We shall come back to this a little later.

It cannot be emphasized strongly enough that self-liberation, or the transition from the dualistic to the unitive state, cannot come about by accumulated knowledge and theoretical understanding, by study or aiming at an outer goal. It cannot come by wanting to be different, by striving to attain a state that does not already exist within. It can come only by being in the now, by discovering that everything already exists within, behind the levels of confusion and pain. And this state behind the acutely, momentarily experienced state can be liberated and brought to the surface only when the level of confusion and pain is totally understood.

The natural cosmic flow, existing within the psyche of every living being, in everything that lives around and within yourself, is a powerful bubbling life stream, carrying you automatically and naturally toward the state of self-realization where there is no longer any opposition and painful conflict. This is the natural state, so you have nature on your side. By entrusting yourself to the life stream, by allowing yourself to perceive it, you will facilitate the unfolding of your natural destiny.

The most insignificant problem can show you how you embrace error and opposition, a no-current, out of fear and ignorance. It can show how you stop the natural cosmic movement of which you are an integral part and which is an integral part of you. Only by a very personalized look at your reactions to daily occurrences can you make these words a personally experienced truth. It cannot happen by paying lip service to the principle behind them, even if you understand intellectually what I am saying. Intellect will not suffice to bring you to the transition from dualism to unity.

Growth on the dualistic plane must always be fraught with fear of the undesirable opposite. Therefore your growth process will be stunted as long as you view your goal of growth as good, as opposed to bad.

On the unitive plane, growth is not threatened by an opposite; hence it need not be feared, nor opposed. But growth cannot come by opposing the opposition; it comes only when the feared opposite can be envisaged and accepted if need be.

When you no longer fear one opposite, no longer cling fearfully to the other, then, and only then, can you reach the unitive state. But you cannot do so as long as fear is in your heart.

The process of growing into the unitive state means forever increasing unfolding and expansion. It means a widening experience of the infinite possibilities of beauty, life, and goodness. But remember, beauty is not the opposite of ugliness; life is not the opposite of death; good is not the opposite of bad; because in the unitive state they are never threatened by an opposite.

Indications of Increasing Unity

Along the road of transition from the dualistic to the unitive state it is important to understand a few further landmarks, which might help you to understand your own life right now. When you are engaged in intense self-search, when you vigorously confront yourself and face truth upon truth, setting up new inner conditions, your psyche goes through profound upheavals. The painful past state, as you know, was a result of false ideas. As these false ideas begin to crumble, the destruction may bring about more or less drastic outer changes.

When you are in a transition period, it is possible for you on some levels to have reached the beginning of the unitive experience. You feel a deep peace and joy in every moment, regardless of whether the experience accords with the desired good. You perceive that every living moment contains the potential for joy and peace.

Being in truth with yourself, you no longer fear anything, nor do you cling tightly and insist that your good should be given to you. You are then open for the divine source to fill you and convey the reality of life where there is nothing to fear and only good exists. You can reach for this good without urgency and obtain it precisely because you know it is yours. You do not fear missing it because you derive joy from both opposites of the dualistic state. This is, briefly, as well as it can be conveyed at all, the essence of the unitive state.

Now this state can begin to exist partially, particularly in certain areas of any individual's life. You have not yet attained the total transition, the awakening in which you find the truth of life to have always existed for you without needing to fear or struggle for anything. But your emerging awareness eventually brings an increasing unfolding and enrichment into your outer circumstances so harmoniously and organically that it may appear almost coincidental.

The outer improvements may or may not coincide with ideas and ideals you have held on the dualistic plane, but the way you experience these ideas and ideals is entirely different. In other words, your goals may remain unchanged, but your experience of the goals will be different. Also, even when you have not reached a goal, you will not suffer as you did when you perceived reality dualistically. The growth into the unitive state definitely manifests in increasing trust in the self, in life. Growth also brings with it a peaceful joyousness that makes every moment vibrant, interesting, and free from anxiety or boredom. Each moment is rich in possibilities and harbors widening vistas of perception never before experienced.

At the same time you continue to react in the old way — with fear, distrust, anxiety, despair, and tight selfwill — usually in the areas where your psyche is afflicted by images, by neurotic behavior patterns, and misconceptions so deeply engraved that you require more extended and patient work to change your inner picture. This other side very gradually catches up, as it were, with the side that is already very close to and already partly in a new land where light is never threatened by darkness.

Error Must Crumble

You have constructed the old state on a foundation of errors, and this foundation must first crumble before a foundation of truthful concepts can be erected. Structures built on erroneous concepts must inevitably be destroyed. This law points up the falsity of dualism, whose earmark is always the perception that one position is flatly and unchangeably desirable and its opposite as undesirable. Thus you cling to the idea that construction is always good, while destruction is always bad. The unification of these two opposites can come only in the unitive state as both sides are reconciled. To understand the unitive state you must recognize that destruction (of error) can be desirable, and construction (of error) is undesirable.

Now, destruction is always a painful process, whether or not it is desirable. While the edifices of error are being destroyed your life may be upset. You feel inwardly threatened and at a loss. Outwardly, even the apparently desirable aspects of your existence have disappeared and no adequate structure has taken their place. The bigger the erroneous constructs are, the greater the period of upheaval, which is naturally painful. But, my friends, it is painful only because you misunderstand what is happening and assume it to mean relapse and your personal inadequacy. Thus you become discouraged, fall into despair and resist the flow that could carry you into a new state of mind. This state, however, can come about only through the destruction of the old state. Fighting against the organic and desirable movement, you prolong the painful, transitional period— painful primarily because it is misunderstood. You feel, "Here I am, trying so hard, yet look what happens in spite of it all! Everything seems to run like sand between my fingers; I not only fail to find fulfillment, but even the pleasures I had are gone."

When you understand that crumbling of the old structure is desirable because the old way only appeared to give you satisfaction, then you will not cry over something that is actually no loss at all. Nor will you be misled into believing that you have not progressed. This state may be the best possible proof that, to a greater extent than you know, you are evolving into a new reality, but you still block it out because you ferociously refuse to allow your intuition to tell you where the cosmic life stream is carrying you.

Instead, you need to sense deeply that what happens is not a relapse, but rather destruction of the old, a process that actually is the very germ of a new construction. You need to sense that in the act of destroying error, truth reconciles construction with destruction and makes them one movement, instead of two warring opposites. Hence you will no longer be discouraged, nor will you suffer particularly when you do not expect that your life should be different, for you will know that all is as it should, even must, be! For the actual loss or absence of a desired good hurts much less when one does not see this "loss" or absence as a negative sign. But when one believes that "If I were where I should be, things would not happen this way," the loss is much more painful. When, instead, you see this transition period as an organic step toward wholeness, you will find the pain much easier to go through.

This should not be misconstrued to mean that you should not seek an intelligent solution to a particular problem. But when you find all the doors closed and life seems to show you quite clearly, from within yourself as well as from the outside, that you cannot find a solution, then you may rest assured that old structures which were based on the error of dualistic perception are crumbling. When you encourage this in your understanding, you will go with the stream instead of opposing it.

I extend the deep and vigorous wish, coming from the deepest regions of universal consciousness, to reach each and every one of you. It will touch you if you open yourself to this force and unite with it. When you unite with this force within you,

you will not want to oppose truth in any form, and you will want to pursue your inner truth. You will begin to feel the effects of this power only later, but it is nevertheless very real, constantly flowing deep within you.

Be in peace, be in that deep region of yourself where all is one.

CHAPTER 8

The Cosmic Pull
Toward Union

Greetings, my dearest friends. A great stream of divine strength and blessings flows around you as a powerful force. Be aware of this force, attune yourself to it, and you will perceive its reality. With its help, a deep understanding of this lecture will enable you to make another step forward on your path toward finding yourself.

There is a great pull in the manifest universe in which you live. This pull is part of the creative principle. Since every individual consciousness is also part of the same creative principle, is made of the same substance in fact, this pull must exist in every individual. It is directed toward union, as the term is usually used, but the term can lose its meaning from over-use. What does union really mean? What does union with God, or with the divine self, really mean? What does union with another individual mean? How does this apply to a human being?

First, the whole plan of evolution aims at uniting individual consciousnesses. Union as a cerebral process, or with an intangible God, is not really union. Only the actual contact of one individual with another establishes the requisite conditions in the personality for true inner union. Therefore this pull toward unity manifests as a tremendous force, moving individuals toward each other, making separateness painful and empty. The life force therefore consists not only of the pull toward others, but also of pleasure supreme. Life and pleasure are one. Lack of pleasure is the distortion of the life force and comes from opposing the creative principle. Life, pleasure, contact and oneness with others are the goal of the cosmic plan.

The pull toward unity aims to bring you out of seclusion. It moves toward contact and melding. To follow the cosmic pull is therefore blissful; it is exhilarating and, at the same time, peaceful. Individual consciousness opposes this force, however, out of the erroneous idea that giving in to it means annihilation. Thus you put yourself in the paradoxical position of believing that life comes from opposing life. Consequently, you live in a very deep conflict — deeper than the psychological problems you uncover in the course of self-exploration.

All of these psychological issues are valid in themselves, as far as they go. They may be negative childhood experiences, misinterpretations of childhood events, hurts and fears you have not properly understood and assimilated. All this must be explored in order to meet and face a deeper, universal, metaphysical conflict — the one I am discussing. The conflict exists because this pull cannot be eliminated. It is the evolutionary force itself, the reality in all that lives and breathes. It permeates every particle of existence and must thus also exist deep in your psyche, whether or not you are aware of it.

Fear of the Pull Toward Union

The conflict arises from fear of and opposition to this pull; the personality resists the natural flow. To the degree that, consciously or unconsciously, you equate the life force with annihilation, you struggle against life itself.

This is the most profound reason for your misconceptions, false fears and guilts, negativity and destructiveness. Deep within, you know that you distrust the greatest spiritual force and thus life itself. The distrust creates a deep guilt that often manifests on the surface as unjustified guilts you cannot give up.

The conflict also manifests as a fear of your deepest instincts so that you cannot ever relax and be unguarded about yourself. Since you are part of the life you distrust, you must also distrust your own innermost self. This is why people insist on dividing body and spirit and why the dualistic concept is perpetuated from generation to generation. You seem to find your salvation in this very division because through it you can justify your rejection of the life principle as it manifests within you. You thus stamp that which you fear as wrong and bad, while claiming that the denial of your very nature is right and good. You justify this irrational attitude by pointing to the most distorted manifestations of the life principle, of the pleasure current, as though they were proof of its badness. Thus people have preached through the centuries that the body is sinful, while the spirit is supposed to be the opposite of the body and therefore good.

It is not true that all your difficulties come from these mis-conceptions, which you embrace as the final spiritual truth. It is closer to the truth that these misconceptions stem from the deep spiritual conflict that motivates you to accuse the great life principle of being the opposite of what it really is.

The misuse of this powerful force by no means proves an acceptance of and trust in it. It is rather a variation on the struggle that ensues when one opposes life with one's own nature. Part of you moves toward others and accepts your instincts and nature, but another side shrinks back from this movement. Deprivation, emptiness, meaninglessness, and a sense of waste ensue. You may then overcompensate by blind-ly, rebelliously, misusing your life force. This leads to pleasure-less experiences and seems to justify your sense of wrongness and danger. Here is truly a kind of life -and-death conflict.

This conflict manifests differently in each individual. But one thing can be said with certainty: the greater the conflict between giving in to the cosmic force and opposing it, the greater the extent of your pain and problems.

If you cannot allow yourself to flow freely with the cosmic stream in the deepest level of your being, you must distort the cosmic stream within you. Since you oppose and distrust the cosmic force, and since the cosmic force manifests within your-self, you do not trust yourself. But if you are to trust yourself and your own innermost nature, you must first trust the pull toward unity. Therefore when you separate nature from the divine principle, or your own innermost nature from spiritual trust, you are engaged in the greatest error, leading to the great-est of confusions. For how could nature, including the depth of your own nature, be opposed to the divine evolutionary plan?

It is the counter-pull in this struggle that creates layers which seem to justify your distrust of your instinctual self. Only the courage to explore these layers within yourself will lead you to the truth of your underlying core, which is wholly trustworthy. But this, as I said, can be experienced only when the deep pull of nature, of evolution, of the creative principle, is understood. Although the intellectual understanding is helpful at first, it is less important than the intuitive understanding, for only intu-itive understanding will allow you to dissolve this conflict.

The conflict congests the creative force, which is compatible with you and your destiny. Even though you block and oppose the pull, you nevertheless cannot avoid it.   It always leads toward contact with others.   Strong fear of such contact leads some individuals into temporarily withdrawing.   Of course, withdrawal can take many forms: It can manifest in your outer life and behavior, but it can also manifest in a much more subtle form.   Outwardly you may engage in contacts but inwardly you remain uninvolved, isolated, separate.   This isolation cannot be maintained for long, because ultimately it will become unbearable.   Nothing that opposes the life principle can be maintained forever.   After all, the life principle represents ultimate reality, and fear of it is based on illusion.   Illusion cannot be maintained indefinitely.   The anxiety arising out of illusion can be eliminated only when this deep conflict is understood and honored and when you finally allow yourself to harmonize with the creative principle.

Even when the opposition is great, the pull toward contact and melding with another must remain, for that is a fundamental fact of creation.   But the counter-pull, with its fear, distrust, and other destructive feelings, must then create negative contact.   All human beings experience some counter-pull, even relatively integrated, healthy individuals.   But let us take the individuals whose counter-pull is relatively weak and whose predominant personality affirms life and their own deepest instincts, and is therefore relatively free of conflict.   Their contact with others will be relatively blissful and unproblematic.   Their pleasure principle will create mutuality, genuine love, and pleasure supreme.

To the degree that opposition to the cosmic pull creates blocks and throws the cosmic stream off course, negative and painful contact has to ensue.   The pleasure principle will be attached to a negative situation, born out of childhood experiences.   This makes fulfillment impossible because the experience of pleasure is always threatened by the attached negativity.   The individual thus becomes a helpless straw between the two pulls, and is driven into painful contact.   Thus the pull toward contact, and the fear of it — which manifests as a pull away from it — are both present.   The latter engenders two fundamental defensive reactions: either the desire to hurt or the sense of being hurt which are inevitable byproducts of the contact.   Since the pleasure principle always remains an element in the life stream, it then necessarily attaches itself to the distorted form of contact.

Negative Pleasure

The pleasure embodied in the greatest force in human life cannot be eliminated, but where this force is distorted, the pleasure becomes negative. Since contact appears to hurt, pleasure manifests either in hurting or in being hurt, to a greater or lesser degree. The connection between hurt and pleasure engenders a vicious circle. The more painfully the pleasure principle of the cosmic pull manifests, the greater the fear, the guilt, the shame, the anxiety, and the tension. Opposition grows, conflict increases, and the vicious circle continues.

The evolutionary problem for every single conscious being is therefore to deeply comprehend and experience this vicious circle without misjudging the negative connection between contact, pain, and the pleasure principle. You must look beyond it by committing to search with an open attitude for your deepest nature. Do not mistake the negative emotions you first encounter for the ultimate reality of your instinctual life.

The layer of destructiveness, blind selfishness, dishonesty, as well as the shameful attachments of the pleasure principle to negative situations, is not your deepest nature. It is merely a demonstration, a result, of this specific conflict, my friends. I cannot emphasize this strongly enough; for when you distrust your innermost nature, you distrust the whole spiritual universe. One cannot exist without the other.

A point comes on the path toward liberation when the problem must be tackled from both ends: Only when you have the courage and honesty to face what you do not like in yourself can you discover that the very energy and substance of these attitudes is essentially constructive and trustworthy. This realization can convert them. Consequently, life's processes will become trustworthy and need no longer be opposed.

Conversely, when you consider the possibility that the entire creative process is trustworthy, you will develop the courage and honesty to transcend the blocks that deform creative energy and divine substance and reconvert them into creativity.

Trust Your Instincts

It is impossible to trust God, to trust life, to trust nature, if one distrusts one's own deepest instincts. For where do these instincts come from? These instincts cannot be crushed, neither can they be denied, uprooted, or forcefully supplanted by foreign elements that seem more palatable to the fearful soul. The only way out is to understand that the innermost instincts are good if they are not interfered with; they are part of the most divine power and not in the least hostile to spiritual growth. Failing to understand this is one of the most tragic errors of humanity, because nothing delays the evolutionary plan as much as this misconception, held by well-meaning and otherwise quite enlightened individuals. These instincts will prove themselves as bearers of light when they are not misjudged, denied, and split off from their divine origin in an artificial duality that presupposes they are evil and regards them as the opposites of divine life, or spiritual life.

So you can come into your own only when you understand this and consequently cease to fear and fight against yourself, your instincts, your body, your nature and against nature as such.

This is the great struggle of humanity. Not knowing this, continuing the blind involvement of the struggle, makes you incapable of relinquishing your separateness. You thus bar yourself from completing your spiritual destiny. You prevent yourself from making peace with your innermost physical and emotional instincts. The peace between body and soul is an inevitable product of self-realization. It is erroneous to believe that the body can simply be left aside in the great venture of integration. When the body is shed before integration has taken place, the integration remains incomplete.

This conflict is so deep and universal that often the most enlightened, evolved, and otherwise unprejudiced individuals become uneasy when they meet it in themselves. Even if they do not conform to small-minded and life-denying views, the deep inner anxiety stemming from this conflict induces them to blind themselves to what goes on within. Whenever your courage falters in facing the conflict — as it manifests nakedly, deep in the recesses of the self — you remain isolated to some extent. You remain involved in painful negativity and split within yourself, until your further evolution brings you to the point where you no longer fear the great stream of which you are a part and which is part of you, leading you toward others and dissolving the wall of separateness and defense. You will then find that not only do you not lose your individuality, but, quite the contrary: You expand and become more yourself.

Now, are there any questions regarding this topic?

QUESTION: You discussed the cosmic pull that becomes negative in the individual at a certain period of his development. Could you explain this further?

ANSWER: When people oppose their cosmic pull and struggle against it, conflict arises. The cosmic pull always remains stronger than the counter-pull, since it is a primary force, while the struggle against it is secondary and superimposed. So you are still pulled toward contact. But your counter-pull denies the primary force, so the negation combines with the original force, and negative contact ensues. The actual contact taking place expresses the pull toward others; the pain arising from it expresses the counter-pull. To the degree you fear the cosmic pull and its destiny, love — which can grow only in a climate of fearlessness — must be absent from the contact. The fear produces defenses, hurts, anger — all these enter the contact and combine with the pleasure principle.

This may manifest on any level of the personality. Negative contact manifesting in the desire to hurt expresses itself in quarrelsomeness, hostility, aggression. On the sexual level, such an individual is sadistic. Negative contact that manifests in being hurt, expresses itself in a tendency to be taken advantage of; you will always manage to put yourself at a disadvantage; you will be driven into damaging behavior patterns. On the sexual level, such an individual is masochistic. Now, of course, no one is simply one or the other; both elements are always represented in a personality, but only one of them may predominate on the surface. For example, just because you fear your cruelty, your need to derive pleasure from hurting others, you may reverse it and direct it against yourself. Since all this takes place on a blind, unconscious level, you do not know what you are doing; you do not know how you are driven, so you are unable to stop the destructive process.

This lecture aims to help you understand that your psychological makeup has a much deeper origin than usually assumed. This deeper origin is the profound, metaphysical conflict in all human beings. When this is perceived and experienced it is much easier to eliminate the psychological distortions that appear to have originated in this life. On the other hand, it must also be realized that the cosmic struggle cannot become even vaguely conscious unless you gain considerable insight into and awareness of your unconscious.

I have given you a topic with which you can again, if you choose to do so, make a deep inroad into your innermost self. Use it, explore it; do not fear your innermost self. Running away from your innermost self is tragic because you inflict upon yourself so much unnecessary pain. Nothing else can ever create as much pain as running away from the self. You have nothing to fear, nothing whatever. Always look deep into yourself, without defensiveness, without anxiety. And the more you look into yourself, the more equipped you will be to establish contact with others. The more you run away from yourself, the more superficial, troublesome, or unsatisfactory such contact must be.

Be in peace, my friends, be blessed, be in God!

Part Four

The Relationship of the Ego to the Real Self

"Life issues a call."

"The call of life is universal in that it aims exclusively at awakening the real self, which is absolute reality."

"The ego blocks the real self."

"Character transformation is an absolute necessity in order to shed the ego identification."

These quotes are all from the first chapter of this section.

The Pathwork teaches that it is essential to learn to trust your deepest instincts because these deepest instincts come from the "real self."

As I try to find my real self and live more in accordance with it, what I most often encounter is that part of me known as the ego — the executive function in me which chooses and plans and systematically tries to maximize my own personal satisfaction. I can often sense that this busy and single-minded executive is not my real self. But what should my attitude toward the ego be?

The ego is an evolutionary development in human beings. We can surmise that in the most primitive Stone-Age peoples, the ego was barely present. Their consciousness was tribal and their self-awareness limited. The sense of being a separate human being was much weaker than it is in us today. As evolution progressed, self-awareness increased. This was necessary and right.

As the millennia and incarnations passed, human beings' consciousness of self developed and expanded. With this came the growing awareness of their individuality, of an "I" apart from the tribe, an "I" that could be referred to both in making day-to-day decisions and in understanding the larger complexities of life. Thus the ego emerged, and brought with it, along with enormous benefits, enormous new challenges for personal and spiritual development.

The fruit of the ego's presence in our modern-day conscious-ness is the clear knowing that *I* am responsible for my life: *all* of my life, the struggles as well as the contentment. This con-viction is absolutely necessary for growth and change to occur. But even after I assent to this truth, there can still be great con-fusion as to what part of me does the positive creating of my life, and what part keeps limiting me. Is my ego the truest and most real me, or is it a selfish and short-sighted barrier to deep-er understanding? Should I cultivate it or uproot it? Or do something else altogether?

The language used by some spiritual paths seems to indicate an attitude that the ego is the enemy. References are made to the need to kill the ego, or vanquish it, or leave it behind.

The position of the Pathwork is somewhat different. The Pathwork states that the problem for most people, at least ini-tially, is that their ego is not strong *enough;* and instructions are given on how to go about strengthening the ego. This is done not for its own sake but rather because only a strong ego has the ability to give itself up in surrender to the leadership of the real self.

A strong ego is one that has learned to be strong in a positive direction, rather than being simply dominating and self-absorbed. Once we have developed a strongly positive ego, the task then is to move beyond the ego and discover that in doing so we can find a source of much greater wisdom and happiness. The ego continues to be a large part of us, but it changes posi-tion. Instead of believing that it is the captain of the ship, it becomes one of the loyal and humble members of the crew.

However, in the initial stages of the transition to the real self, we find that *the ego is highly reluctant to be surpassed.* Indeed, the ego will usually do whatever it can to block the real self from emerging.

So the problem becomes: I am working to change myself. I find that my self is very resistant to that change and seeks to undermine the work at every turn. It sometimes seems that all I have to work with in doing this is the very self which I am also trying to change, and which often is very resistant to being changed.

This is the series of conundrums, boxes within boxes, that eventually confronts all serious travelers on the spiritual path.

This is what makes the task difficult. But the task is not impossible, and we will be shown the way through the impasses and obstacles.

Ultimately, all that is required of us is a *total commitment.* "Only those who consciously and deliberately commit themselves once and for all to living their life for the primary purpose of activating the real self can find the deep inner peace that exists."

D.T.

CHAPTER 9

Responding to the Call of Life

Greetings, my dearest friends. The blessings given are strength and power coming from the sincere wishes and the love of all involved in this venture.

Life issues a call; it makes a demand on every living individual. Most people do not sense this call. Only as you become aware of your own illusions can you simultaneously become more aware of the truth within yourself, and therefore in life. Consequently, you will understand in each moment what the call of life wants to convey to you. How do you respond to it? Do you respond with your total being? Or do you respond half-heartedly? Or do you resist responding at all and make yourself deaf to it? That is the big question, my friends.

The call of life manifests differently to each individual. It is at once universal and intensely personal. It is universal in the sense that it aims exclusively at awakening the real self, absolute reality. It goes about this in a totally unsentimental way. It disregards personal attachments, social considerations, and any other peripheral values, including personal pain or pleasure.

If awakening the real self requires what temporarily seems like destruction, this destruction will turn out to be rather the groundwork of the real inner life, the preparation needed to awaken the inner center. If the awakening brings what also happens to be most joyful to you, the very experience of joy proves that you are more attuned to your real self than you realize.

Moralistic self-defeating attitudes often induce you to reject whatever may lead you to your destiny and self-fulfillment just because it brings joy, since you have the mistaken idea that self-realization must automatically mean deprivation and self-sacrifice. If your life-conditions will not, sooner or later, promote your coming into your real self, they will inevitably be destroyed. Conditions that promote the awakening of the real self bring peace, joy, well-being, and intense pleasure. Such is the stream of life, which is often blocked by humanity's stubborn resistance to seeing it.

The call of life is universal. The attitude necessary to awaken the inner center follows universal values. Truth, love, and beauty are universal aspects of the real life stream. The isolated ego-existence is also a general state affecting all people, but how the ego blocks the real self is a personal question; what is universal is the fact that transformation of one's character is necessary to permit the life stream to flow freely. We shall return to the subject of transformation a little later.

These universal principles can be intellectually recognized, but they are not necessarily felt and experienced. This can happen only when the personal experience of the life stream is recognized and responded to. Therefore, any path leading to genuine self-realization must be intensely personal and has to deal with intensely personal problems.

Those who believe that imbibing general truth and collecting more truthful beliefs can accomplish the goal delude themselves. They do so because they do not want to look at the truth of who they are at the moment; they prefer an idealized notion of themselves. Their very evasion alienates them more from the goal than the honest admission that they do not want to look at themselves, do not want to permit themselves to experience emotions they fear or disapprove of, and above all, do not wish to transform their character defects. The actual — not theoretical — activation of the real self, with its vibrating life, limitless abundance, infinite possibilities for good, and its supreme wisdom and joy, happens to the exact degree that you dare take a look at the temporary truth of yourself. This means feeling what you feel; having the courage to transform yourself into a better human being for no other reason than a desire to contribute to life, rather than to make an impression and grasp for approval. When the immediate barriers to transformation for its own sake are overcome, then the real self with all its treasures will clearly manifest.

Are You Ashamed of What You Are Now?

One of those barriers is shame of what you are now. This shame makes you set up a wall of secrecy that makes you lonely. The loneliness may be denied or rationalized; other circumstances may be blamed. In reality, it is your wish to hide your self from yourself and others that separates you from them. In the deep recesses of your mind you fear that you are different from others, that you are worse than they, and the shame of your difference cannot be exposed. This very secret conviction traps you in the particular illusion of your separateness, depriving you of discovering your universality that offers its healing climate for your psyche. Again, this cannot be accomplished by theoretical understanding, but only by actually experiencing those areas where you still hide yourself. These are precisely the main barriers separating you from the life stream. The solitude of inner secretiveness cannot be relieved, no matter how favorable your outer circumstances. Such loneliness can be relieved only when you overcome the pride hidden by your shame. The intensely personal work of overcoming your pride leads to the realization of the universal values which alone can give you the courage to go with the life stream.

The universal self often contradicts outer rules which come from humanity's ego-self. Hence, no matter how much people rebel against conformity and social laws, they still find themselves confined within the ego-self, deeply immersed in its dualistic struggle of conformity (and the submission it requires) versus rebellion and defiance. True emancipation from the ego's outer rules requires neither conformity nor rebellion. It acts on inner values that may or may not coincide with the dictates of society. In neither case will the person using inner values be damaged. He or she will become more whole, even in a temporary upheaval.

The key is not as hidden as it may seem. Only ask whether you are motivated by love and truth and have totally committed yourself to a course of honesty and integrity in this particular issue, regardless of public opinion. Do you let go of the fear, the pride, the selfwill of your ego and strive toward the voice of the divine within you, again, regardless of appearances? This way is always open, and whenever you choose it, it will emancipate you from the ego-struggle. Its solutions will bring you less pain and anxiety. Answers will inevitably follow that will reconcile your conflict and bring peace.

The call of life disregards the superficial morality most people ardently adhere to or equally ardently fight against. This morality is based on the fear of disapproval. People may fight it because in their minds goodness is equated with deprivation. The call of life disregards outer appearances and shortsighted sentimentality. It surges toward bringing all individuals into their birthright, since it is based entirely on universal values. Everything that matters is contained within it.

Why does humanity put up such a struggle against fulfilling its destiny, when such destiny brings nothing but good? Why do you resist hearing the call of your life stream when it brings you all that is safe, good, productive, and joyful? This is the tragic battle of humanity. On the one hand, you are very disturbed by the insecurity of your existence. You sense the waste of your life as long as you pay exclusive allegiance to the outer self, and therefore to outer values. On the other hand, you do everything in your power to maintain your unhappy state. In fact, you seek more and more means to reinforce your ego-identification: more outer ways, outer activities, outer beliefs, and outer escapes. At times you may succeed only in making yourself deaf to the voice from deep within. At other times, you feel the deep unrest, but you refuse to understand it.

You Need to Commit Completely

Only those who consciously and deliberately make the decision and commit themselves once and for all to living their life for the primary purpose of activating the real self can find the deep inner peace that exists even while inner errors still prevent total self-realization.

Let every one of you who reads these words question why you are on this path. What is your aim in life? Do you live just to make do as best you can? Do you work on this path because there are certain symptoms you wish removed which you feel interfere unpleasantly with your life? Certainly, you are free to do so. But realize the deeper meaning of this. For as long as you aim solely to remove certain effects of identifying with your ego because you ignore or fear the activation of the real self, other symptoms of this principal disease will appear. Total well-being cannot be accomplished, even if you succeed in removing temporary states of pain and deprivation. There is a vast difference between these two goals. As long as you fail to orient yourself completely toward activating your real self, you cannot know real safety, peace, and well-being. Nor can you use the storehouse of potential within yourself, or experience your freedom to use the unlimited resources of the universe for your benefit. Not being able to do any of this, not being able to be what you can be, is an endless pain that you need to allow yourself to experience consciously in order to have the incentive to do something about it.

By contrast, the pursuits of the ego, no matter how great your accomplishments, will never give you peace and security, nor the sense of being the best you can be. The ego-drive may appear to give you power over others, but it cannot ever give you autonomy and independence, so that, sooner or later, the illusion of power over others is exposed as fake.

I advise all those who seek help to define your aim very clearly. What is your aim? How far do you wish to go? Do you commit yourself completely? Then visualize the specific symptoms you wish to remove. Any disturbance is merely a symptom of the basic ill of exclusive ego-identification, no matter what name you give it: neurosis, sickness, distortion, unhappiness. You are free merely to remove symptoms. Consider what the removal of the symptoms alone means for your future. What can you envisage afterwards? Can you envisage that more is possible? What is this more? How would your life be with this more? Or do you commit yourself totally to finding who you really are, what is possible for you?

I believe that those who really think about it and properly grasp the whole meaning of this important question, clearly questioning themselves without delusions, will respond to life with their total being. Let us discuss this commitment to the real self.

Perhaps you have experienced to some degree through certain meditations that the universe contains unlimited good, available to you if you open yourself to it. There are times when you vividly experience this truth and you know, without the shadow of a doubt, that your experience is not coincidence nor illusion; you know it to be a fact. When this is so, your entire attitude is clear, free, and relaxed. You are deeply convinced of your truth and trust it; you feel deserving and hence do not cringe from fulfillment; hence it comes. Your whole being resonates with a positive, constructive vibration without any conflict. You do not feel selfish for wishing to experience beauty, nor do you withhold the best of yourself.

But then there are also those occasions when things do not work that way. Even though in certain areas of your life you have already experienced such positive manifestations, in other areas you cannot break through. Trying to attain this undifferentiated good with your ego-self does not work. Where your real self is blocked, the doors to the benign universe are closed. This is not because some forbidding authority decided that you are not worthy of this or that particular fulfillment; it is simply because something within you bars the way, and this something has to be found so you can eliminate it.

Whatever the obstruction is, it makes you fear letting go of the ego, so you remain centered in, and oriented to, the ego. This ego is incompatible with the unified world of all good since it is split off from it in duality. It can be open only to partial good, to which there exists — as always in dualities — another, undesirable, side. This undesirable side may weaken the wish for the good —entirely unconsciously. Also, whatever stands in the way of letting go of the ego is always, when fully exposed and understood, something that impairs one's integrity and deforms the character structure. Hence, the deep inner conscience feels undeserving of all good and cringes from it. That very unsureness of integrity makes the personality unable to cope with the good even where it exists.

Only the total self can relate to and unite with total good. You can test this right now. Take any problem you are working on, be it an outer problem you wish changed, or an inner condition you wish to overcome. Meditate, expand yourself, and reach for the total goal. Claim this total goal. How often does it happen that you feel it is impossible to do so! Test it right now.

Although you really want to claim your goal, you still feel it is impossible. There is some wall that does not let you get through. This wall must never, under any circumstances, be disregarded or glossed over. You must never use pressure from your will to overcome the "no" of this wall. Such forcing will remove you further from your real self within and hence from the reality of the life where all good is available. Instead, you have to interpret the meaning of the wall. Translate it into clear words. Whether you doubt that you can have your goal, or feel guilty about getting it, or have a sense of not deserving it, or are afraid of life's demands when you do have it, these still do not add up to the final answer. This reservation within yourself must be linked with a character defect you have not really faced, nor do you wish to, because you do not want to abandon it.

Character transformation is an absolute necessity in order to shed the ego-identification. When I say "shed," I do not mean it in the sense of giving the ego up but of using it as a tool to find the inner being, and then allowing the ego to integrate with it. It should be clearly understood that such integration is possible only when certain character defects have been already transformed or when the person is truly willing to transform them in all sincerity and without subterfuge. There must be a total commitment, without pretense or play-acting. When this is your total response to life, the life stream will become discernible and its wise guidance and meaningfulness will become a powerful presence in your life.

The Deep Conflict of Dualism

Now, why are you so afraid of this total commitment to life? Of relinquishing ego-identification? Of the positive manifestations that can enrich you? Why do you resist the good and battle to maintain painful struggle and insoluble conflict? Why do you fear the good that liberates you? And why do you put your faith in the imprisoning ego of the little outer self and the little outer values? There are several answers to these questions, depending on the angle. Let us first choose the following approach.

When you doubt a larger reality and do not take a chance on it, you stay in a world of duality. As you know, this dualistic world is characterized by the following conflict: "If I am unselfish, I must suffer. I do not want to suffer. But if I am selfish, I will be rejected, despised, not loved, left alone. And that is suffering too." In this struggle you go back and forth, seeking a solution. The more you believe in the inevitable "truth" of these two alternatives, the more you are bound to experience life according to them. You do not dare to be unselfish; you cannot wholly want to be unselfish since it means giving up what you believe is personal fulfillment and happiness. Nor can you fully commit yourself to a life of selfishness —partly due to the ever-present existence of your real self, partly because you fear the world's opinion. This is the tragedy of this senseless struggle. You cannot extricate yourself from its meshes as long as you identify with and entrust yourself to the values, rules, and concepts of ego-logic.

When you want to be transformed, you must want to give up selfishness and the desire to cheat life, yourself, and others. You cannot wholly risk this when it spells the sacrifice of all you want. But the most painful state is indecision, and this holds true on all levels. It is your fate as long as you have not transcended the ego level of reality. You cannot reconcile fulfillment and unselfishness, so you remain undecided; you continue to vacillate between two camps. If many people were totally capable of committing themselves to a life of selfishness, they would soon come out of it because they would recognize that it leads nowhere, that it does not lead to the salvation they half-heartedly seek in both camps.

You are all in this struggle, every one of you. All your problems are an expression and direct outcome of this duality. Look at your problems, go deeply enough into them, and you will see that this is so. You fear the impulses of the larger, wiser self, but cannot want to commit yourself to it wholeheartedly as long as you believe that some disadvantage will result from your decision.

That you are capable of reaching for and receiving the good of the universe only when your defects are being overcome may, at first glance, appear like the concept of reward and punishment. I might say that this concept is a distortion of the process I have explained. Reward and punishment presuppose an outer authority who hands out the just deserts of the individual's actions and attitudes. Reward or punishment are often presumed to take place only in a hereafter.

You Cannot Have the Best Unless You Give It

What I explain, however, is a mechanism taking place within the personality. The innermost self is aware of the incongruity of reaching for the best while refusing to give the best. Moreover, obtaining the best is a burden one fears when one is not willing to also give the best. Conversely, giving one's best is impossible when one associates it with sacrifice and disadvantage. The very existence of a belief in punishment and reward covers up the deep despair that unselfishness brings deprivation, so one is forced to hold back the total desire to love and to give. Rewards and punishments, in whatever forms they exist, are compensations for the unbearable reality perceived in duality.

When the real self is activated, this conflict no longer exists. It is possible to activate the real self when this particular conflict in you is brought out of hiding. Inside the reality of the inner center, this split no longer exists. You will find that it is equally possible to give of yourself wholeheartedly, to love, to be unselfish, to be humble, to relinquish the egocentricity of the frightened child, to allow others to be free no matter what this means for you, and yet not be a loser. Soon the feeling of not necessarily having to be a loser will change into a conviction that being a winner is possible. First, you will understand that

being a winner is possible; later, that it is inextricably connected with decency. This will be so because you are free enough to
want both.

When you take on the transformation of your defects, you
will like yourself sufficiently to open yourself to all the good
that wants to come to you. When you begin to succeed in this
transformation you will be strong enough to stand happiness.
You can claim the best when you are in the process of transforming whatever makes you dislike yourself, whether or not
you are aware of this self-dislike, whether or not you are still
projecting your self-hate onto others. Then you will realize the
truth of absolute reality and of your real self, which is that there
is no limit to expansion. Through this unfoldment your intuition will become strong and reliable. You will then heed the
demand of your personal life stream. You will have the courage
to go with it whether or not it seems to conform with outer
expectations, rules, and values. As long as you are very determined to follow the inner values, the outer values will cease to
be important, either in your own mind or in the outer manifestation of your life. You will therefore no longer fear when your
life does not conform to convention. Soon outer life will follow
suit and no friction will accrue. The world will fall into step
with you.

The Two Important Keys

There are two important keys for you in this lecture, which
may be the very points you seek in order to come out of a
momentary bottleneck. I recapitulate them briefly:

1. What is your aim in life? What is your aim on this path?
How far do you wish to go? Do you want to remove only a few
symptoms? Or do you wish total self-realization, the activation
of an inner center in which all good, salvation from anxiety,
insecurity, and confusion, exist? If so, are you willing to pay the
price of perseverance, of total commitment? The total commitment brings out your total possibilities. The unlimited potentials of your innermost being enable you to realize unlimited good.

2. Find the exact point where your positive wishes are
blocked, and then question what particular character defect
does not permit you to abandon a self-destructive, self-denying
attitude. State clearly that you wish to find it. Once you see it,
there is still time to decide whether or not you want to give it
up. If you do not, find out why not. The insistence upon hold-

ing on to something that violates your integrity and your decency holds back the best you have to offer and the best you can be. This impairs your self-respect. It may not be a crass outer manifestation; it may be a hidden little deviation that does not seem to harm anyone, but it always does, whether or not you are aware of it.

The progress that is vividly experienced by some of you is in exact proportion to your willingness and openness. There is no mystery about what brings the progress, for this path must work when willingness and openness exist. Those of you who are not satisfied with your progress should question yourselves deeply and sincerely: "Where have I held back? Where did I not want to go all the way? Where have I lost the clarity of the aim? And where have I disconnected the aim from where I am at this moment because I do not want to expose myself?" You avoid seeing that you hold back in fear and shame; they are unnecessary obstacles you use to barricade the doors to liberation.

Those of you who have progressed and sense the excitement of a new life to come have much more to look forward to, for you will now fortify your own powers. You will be able to activate them more and more to remove the obstacles of your remaining illusions and to orient yourself to what is eternal within yourself, what is never conflicted or tortured. You will learn to experience it as a living reality.

Be blessed. Receive the strength and the love that stream forth. Be in peace. Be in God!

CHAPTER 10

The True Function
of the Ego

Greetings, my dearest friends. May blessings and strength, understanding of truth, and vital flow of universal energy fill and sustain you.

Awareness of Our Fears

Many of my friends on this intensive path of self-realization have come to a crossroads where they see the old inner landscape, which is fear: fear of life, fear of death, fear of pleasure, fear of giving up control, fear of feelings —fear of *being,* as such. It takes considerable self-confrontation, as you all know, to be aware of these fears. They are usually covered up, but they exist nevertheless.

As awareness of these fears increases, one gradually and automatically also becomes aware of the effects these heretofore unconscious fears have on one's life — what they make one do and how they make one withdraw from living. One then begins to understand those vague feelings of missing out on life that one usually has without quite knowing why, and one begins to realize how much one misses.

The source of all these fears is a misunderstanding of the function of the ego and its relation to the real self. This relation is extremely subtle and difficult to put into words, for, as with all truths of life, it is full of apparent contradictions to the extent that you find yourself thinking and living dualistically. The moment you transcend this dualism, two opposite and apparently mutually exclusive aspects become equally true. This applies to the ego in relation to the real self. It is true when one says the ego's predominance, its exaggerated strength, is the greatest hindrance to productive living. And it is equally true when one says a weak ego is incapable of establishing healthy living.

Ignorance of the Real Self

Humanity's unhappy condition is due primarily to ignorance about the real self. At best, the more enlightened human beings accept its existence as a philosophical precept, but this is completely different from the experience — the living, dynamic experience —of its existence. If people were educated with the idea and the goal that they contain something deep within themselves that is infinitely superior to the ego-self, they would be given the opportunity, by experimentation and exploration, to seek communication with this nucleus. They would become able to reach their true inner being.

Since this is not the case, people become more and more limited in their concepts and goals. They ignore that there is anything else alive in them besides the ego. Even those of you who have, for years, formed a concept of the real self, of the creative substance that enlivens every human being, forget in ninety-five percent of your daily lives that this creative being lives and moves in you and you live and move in it. You forget its existence. You do not reach for its wisdom. You stake all your reliance on your limited outer ego-self. You neglect to open yourself to the deeper self's truth and feelings. You go blithely ahead as though there really were nothing else but your conscious mind, your ego-self with its immediately accessible thinking processes and will-force. With that attitude you short-change yourself greatly.

Such forgetfulness inevitably has various consequences. The first one is the question of identification. When you identify yourself exclusively with the ego or outer conscious self, when your sense of self is predominantly associated with the ego functions, you become completely imbalanced and your life becomes emptied of substance and meaning. Since the ego cannot replace, or in any way come near, the resourcefulness of the real self, it is inevitable that such people — and they comprise the majority of human beings — become tremendously frightened and insecure. They must feel inadequate, and their sense of life, of living, of self must become very flat and unenjoyable. Substitute pleasures are then, often frantically, looked for — pleasures that are hollow and leave them exhausted and dissatisfied.

The ego cannot add deep feelings and a deep flavor to living. Nor can it produce profound and creative wisdom. The ego can only memorize, learn, collect other people's creative knowledge, repeat, and copy. It is equipped to remember, to sort out, to select, to make up the mind, to move in a certain direction — outward or inward. These are its functions. But it is not the ego's function to feel, to experience deeply and to know deeply, which is to be creative. When I say creative, I do not merely mean artistically creative. Every simple act of living can be creative, provided you are activated by the real self. Every act is uncreative when you are cut off from the real self, no matter how much effort you put into it.

Let us come back to those fundamental human fears I listed before and consider them in the light of this information. As I said, these fears come into being as a result of cutting off from the real self and remaining in ignorance, living with false ideas. Let us begin with the fear of death, since it is this particular fear that casts such a shadow into everyone's life. If you identify predominantly with your ego, your fear of death is really quite justified, for the ego dies indeed. This may sound like a frightening statement for those who have not yet experienced the truth and reality of their inner being. It is frightening precisely for the reason I just mentioned, namely, that a sense of being, of existing, a sense of self, exists for so many by identifying only with the ego. This is why no human being who has activated his real self and experiences it as a daily reality is ever afraid of death. One feels and knows one's immortal nature, one is filled with its eternal quality; it can only be a continuum, for this is its inherent nature. This cannot be explained by the logic the ego is used to; such logic is much too limited to comprehend this.

I want to add here that an intellectual acceptance of the real self as a philosophical precept will not alleviate fear of death because it cannot give a sense of reality and true experience of the real self. This requires more. It requires an actualization of the faculties of the real self.

Fear of Life and Pleasure

The next fear on the list would be fear of life. Whoever fears life must fear death, and whoever fears death must fear life, because they are really both the same. This statement can also be truly understood only when one experiences the real self, which reconciles all apparent opposites. Then one sees that life and death are the sunny and the shadow sides of a certain manifestation of consciousness, nothing more nor less.

Now, the fear of life is justified when one's sense of identification is exclusively attached to the ego. For the ego's capacities to cope with life and to live life productively are extremely limited. In fact, they are downright insufficient and must leave the individual uncertain, insecure, inadequate. The real self, on the other hand, always has answers, always has solutions, no matter what the problem is; it always makes any experience, regardless of how unnecessary and futile it may seem at first, a deeply meaningful stepping stone toward further expansion. It increases the experience of life and the realization of one's inherent potentials. It therefore has the capacity to render you more alive, more fulfilled, and steadily stronger.

Certainly, none of this can be said about the ego. The ego is constantly ensnared in apparently insoluble situations, problems, and conflicts. The ego is adapted exclusively to the level of duality: this versus that, right versus wrong, black versus white, good versus bad. As you know, this is inadequate for approaching most of life's problems. Apart from the fact that no truth can be found if one looks at one side as black and the other as white, the dimensions of these problems include many other considerations. The ego is incapable of transcending the dualistic level, of bringing into harmony the truth of both sides, as it were. Therefore it cannot find solutions and is perpetually trapped and anxious. Thus, an ego identification automatically brings fear of life in its wake.

The next on the list might be fear of pleasure. For those of you whose self-exploration is still not extremely deep, such a statement may sound absolutely incredible —just as fear of happiness would. You would then say to yourself, "This has no application to me." But let me tell you that everyone — to the degree they feel unhappy, unfulfilled, and empty — fears happiness, fulfillment, and pleasure, no matter how much they strain and yearn for it on the conscious level. It must be so; it is the equation that must come out even. Your life demonstrates the fact, for your life is never a product of circumstances beyond your control, or of causes beyond those you inwardly set in motion. It is always a product of your own inner consciousness.

Fear of pleasure, of happiness, of fulfillment, is a reality applicable to all human beings. At first, it is only a question of connecting consciously with this fear. The moment you do so, you will then, at last, understand why your life does not yield what another part of you so ardently wishes. The more the ego cramps up to get what you want consciously, forgetting that it is not the ego alone that can attain it, the less can fulfillment be possible.   Yet it is not the conscious ego that necessarily obstructs it, but some other part of your being, which is neither the ego nor the real self.   However, the conscious ego is often blindly driven to act the way the unconscious, fearful, life-refusing part dictates.   This is then rationalized and explained away.   Even when one pays allegiance only to the active ego-self with its consciousness, even then the ego-self is no more than an obedient agent, whether you know it or not.   The question is only whether the ego follows erroneous destructive drives or whether it is activated by the real self.

Hence, it is absolutely essential that you be open to your own inner reactions which shrink from happiness and pleasure.   To understand this in context, I should like to say to you now: if you derive your sense of self only from the ego faculties, giving up the ego must seem terribly frightening.   And right here is where you are caught in an insoluble conflict as long as you remain stuck in it: Unfoldment and pleasure, delight and creative living, fulfillment and happiness, can exist only when the real self is activated, when you do not identify exclusively with the ego, but when you are connected and identified with the real self, with the eternal, creative substance of your being. Achieving this necessitates letting go of the direct ego controls.   It requires trust and courage to surrender to an inner movement that is not responsive to the outer thinking and willing faculties.

It is easy to ascertain the truth of this statement when you ponder a minute the heightened moments in your life. Whatever was truly pleasurable, inspired, effortless, fearless, creative, and deeply joyful was precisely due to this letting go and being animated by something other than the usual faculties under the direct determination of the outer self.   Then happiness is not only possible but is a natural byproduct.   You cannot be the real self without being happy, and you cannot be happy unless you are integrated with, and enlivened by, the real self. This is the kind of happiness that knows no fear of ending or loss or unwelcome byproducts.   It is the kind of happiness that is, at one and the same time, dynamic, stimulating, exciting, vibrantly alive, and yet peaceful.   There is no longer any split from separating these concepts and making them mutually exclusive, which is what the dualistic ego does.   In the split way of experiencing life, peacefulness excludes excitement and brings boredom.   Excitement excludes peace and brings anxiety and tension.   You are confronted, as in so many other instances, with a choice that is no longer necessary when you enter the realm of the unified real self.

How can you fearlessly embrace a state that must dispense with the ego faculties when your sense of being alive seems to come exclusively from these ego faculties? This is just where you are trapped. Unless you see your fear of happiness in this light, you will not find your way out of this trap. You will be constantly vacillating. On the one hand, you will be terrified of letting go of the ego. On the other, you will be constantly in a state of greater or lesser hopelessness that may be more or less conscious. A feeling of missing out on your life, of lacking something essential, will haunt you, because what is necessary to alleviate this condition cannot come about until you let go of the ego's predominance.

Only gradually do you become acclimated to the new condition, the new vibrations, the new ways of the real self's functioning. But this is certainly not incompatible with living in a body on this earth sphere. Not at all. It merely means harmonious interaction between the ego and the real self. It means knowing the ego's functions, its limitations, as well as its power.

The Wisdom and Ecstasy of the Life Force

The real self exudes and transmits a vital flow of energy, consisting of many distinct streams. It is what I usually call the life force. This life force is not only a tremendous power, it is *consciousness*. It contains deep wisdom and inexorable lawfulness, eternal and immutable. It is necessary to explore and understand these laws. Such understanding enriches life in a most wondrous manner, to a degree you cannot imagine.

Denying the intense ecstasy of this life force, which manifests in some areas more intensely than in others on all levels of existence, means courting various degrees of death. Embracing this life force means living deathlessly. The denial of the pleasure supreme of life is death. The fact that the ego came into existence means that death came into existence. The ego is a split-off particle of the vaster consciousness, which still remains in all people. Unless this split-off part is integrated with its origin, it dies. Therefore splitting off and dying are related, as reunification and living are related and interdependent. Ego existence, pleasurelessness, and death are directly connected, as the real self, pleasure supreme, and life are directly connected. Therefore whoever fears letting go of the ego, who fears and denies pleasure because of this fear, must court death. This is the true meaning of death. It is a denial of the true, original life kernel.

All this, my friends, may lead to the misunderstanding that the ego should be dispensed with. Unfortunately, many a spiritual teaching has made this error and thus brought confusion to its adherents. Doing this would merely lead to the opposite extreme, and both extremes are always equally wrong, damaging, and dangerous.

People who have throughout a lifetime — nay, often during several lifetimes —overemphasized the ego, in the mistaken idea that it is not only safety but life itself, become tired. They become tired because every soul movement based on misconceptions is exhausting by its very nature.

The various false ways of relief from a cramped ego always mean the weakening of the ego. If, on the one hand, the ego is too strong, it inevitably must be too weak on the other. I put this in practical terms for you who are working on this path: To the extent that you are frightened of letting go of ego control because you believe the false idea that letting go makes you lose strength, to that extent you are unable to assert yourself because you are afraid. The more capable you are of self-surrender to your feelings, to the creative process, to the unknown qualities of life itself, to a mate —the stronger you must be. You will then not fear to make decisions, to make mistakes, to meet difficulties. You will rely on your own resources, will have the integrity of your own views, will pay the price for selfhood, will assert your rights as you fulfill your obligations freely and willingly, not out of fear of authority or of the consequences of disapproval. The ego strength of such healthy self-assertion makes self-surrender possible.

Conversely, the weakness of an ego that fears self-responsibility makes self-surrender, and thus pleasure, impossible. The person who habitually overcharges and exhausts the ego faculties will then seek false relief. Such false relief can take many forms. One form is insanity, where the ego is completely disabled. In severe cases it takes the form of neurotic manifestations, where the ego is unable to use its faculties of strength, selfhood, and self-responsibility. Or it can take the form of alcoholism, drug addiction, and all the artificial ways of obtaining relief from an overtense ego that is deprived of pleasure because it is too frightened to surrender to the creative process.

The Ego as a Proper Servant

It is therefore of primary importance to comprehend what the ego faculties are, how to use them, and where the ego's limitations are. We shall go into greater detail in the future; all I want to say at the moment is this: The ego must know that it is only a servant to the greater being within. Its main function is to deliberately seek contact with the greater self within. It must know its position. It must know that its strength, potentiality, and function is to decide to seek contact, to request help from the greater self, to establish contact permanently with it. Moreover, the ego's task is to discover the obstructions that lie between it and the greater self. Here, too, its task is limited. The realization always comes from within, from the real self, but it comes as a response to the ego's wish to comprehend and to change falseness, destructiveness, error. In other words, the ego's task is to formulate the thought, the intent, the desire, the decision. But its limitation is in the execution of the thought, the intent, the desire.

After the ego has fulfilled its task of deciding for truthfulness, integrity, honesty, effort, and good will, it must step aside and allow the real self to come forth with its intuition and inspiration that set the pace and direct the individual path. The ego must, again and again, select, decide, intend, in order to follow this development. It must be willing to learn from within and to comprehend the deeper language of the unconscious, which is first quite obscure but later becomes increasingly more obvious. It must learn to interpret the messages of the destructive unconscious, as well as of the still more deeply unconscious real self, with all its wonderful creativity and constructiveness. The ego must lend its wholehearted support, its one-pointed effort, its most constructive attitude and undivided attention to the inner path. It must know its limitation as to the deep wisdom, the individual rhythm of the path, the timing, the strength to persevere in difficult times, and call upon the unlimited resources of the real self. It must develop a finesse to sense the subtle interplay between the increasingly alert ego and the increasingly more manifest real self, so that it may learn when to be strong and assertive in overcoming resistance, in disclosing excuses and rationalizations, and when to step aside in a more passive, listening and learning attitude. The ego can be likened to hands and arms that move toward the source of life and stop moving when their function is no longer anything else but to receive.

May you all truly benefit by this lecture. Meditate with the wish to make use of it, not only by understanding it theoretically, but by truly seeking that part of yourself that is eternal, that is truly adequate, and that is always in wonderful, ecstatic delight. For this is your birthright.

Be in peace, be blessed, be in God!

CHAPTER 11

The Phenomenon
of Consciousness

Greetings, my dearest friends. Love, truth and blessings are given to you in rich abundance. Open your innermost channels and let the flow stream from and into you. In this lecture I wish to deal with the phenomenon of consciousness, which is so difficult to explain to the human state of consciousness.

Consciousness permeates all being, all creation, all existence — everything that is. In your dualistic realm, you speak of consciousness and energy as if they were two separate phenomena. This is incorrect. Consciousness is a creator of energy, and energy must contain various aspects of consciousness, perhaps "variations" of consciousness, as well as degrees. There is no physical, biological, electrical or atomic energy that could be anywhere near as potent as the energy of direct consciousness. By this I mean the energy of thought, feeling, intent, attitude, belief.

Thought is Energy and Has Feeling

Every thought is energy. You experience this energy as feeling. There cannot be a thought —even the most mechanical, dead, sterile, cut-off thought —that does not also contain feeling. Pure, abstract thought may appear to be totally divorced from feeling content. This is not so. As a matter of fact, the more abstract and pure the thought is, the more the feeling must be commensurate with it. You must also differentiate between cut-off thought and abstract thought. Don't confuse them. Cut-off thought is a defense against feelings and undesirable aspects of the self. Abstract thought is a result of a highly integrated, spiritual state. But even the former can never be divorced from feeling —that is, energy content. The underlying feeling might be fear, apprehension, anxiety about the complexity of what the self suspects to exist and wishes to avoid.

Self-hate, and a variety of other feelings which you well know, may co-exist with this.

As its underlying energy current, abstract thought contains a feeling of immense peace, of an intrinsic understanding of universal law that is bound to induce joyousness and bliss. A purely abstract thought would create this kind of energetic or feeling experience. The more subjective the thought is, the more tinged with negativity the feeling becomes. A subjective thought is one that is created from personal desire and personal fear, from a state of egotism and separation — me versus the other. It is therefore never in truth.

Let us, for example, examine desire. In the realm of duality, like everything else, desire fulfills a dual role. Desire, from a spiritual point of view, may be "undesirable." For too much desire, intense desire, subjective desire — desire stemming from the ego and its distortions — alienates you from the core of your being. Such desire often contains pride, selfwill, fear, lack of trust in the universe. It creates a tense, contracted energy system and prevents the flow of the life force. Hence spiritual teachings often advocate a state of desirelessness as a necessary prerequisite for connecting with the divine self. It is a state to be cherished for spiritual self-realization.

At the same time, it is equally true that if there is no desire, there cannot be expansion. There cannot be venturing out into new ground, into new realizations and states of awareness. There can be no development and no purification. For what would motivate an individual to muster the courage, perseverance and steadfastness necessary to grope one's way out of darkness and suffering? Only desire does. This kind of desire contains courage, patience, commitment, and faith in the possibility of attaining a better state.

Here you have a typical example of a dualistic confusion that arises when you say that it is either right or wrong to have desire, depending on which aspect of it you perceive. You can transcend the painful, confusing and limited state of dualistic consciousness only when you see beyond the either/or and see the true and distorted possibilities of both apparent opposites. The moment you see this, opposites exist no longer. You then pass into a deeper and wider state of consciousness, in which you comprehend beyond the limited dualistic state. This applies to many manifestations of your life. Rarely if ever is anything in itself good or bad. It depends on how it manifests, what the true underlying motivations are. Desire must exist in the human heart in order to overcome the hurdles, the temptations to self-deceit, which block the way to the abstract knowledge of the universe. This does not mean, I repeat, abstraction in the sense of mechanical, dead, alienated, superficial, unfeeling or defensive thinking.

How can knowledge, how can knowing — which is consciousness — be unfeeling? Even unfeeling knowing, what you call in this era "intellectual knowledge," must have a feeling content. It stirs up certain chain reactions. And even though such knowledge may be fragmented, and though people may use it to get away from the energy or feeling aspect of living, it nevertheless contains feeling, as I mentioned before, although they may not recognize these feelings. So, consciousness is always a feeling, an energy manifestation, whether or not you are aware of it. Even the most mechanical, fragmented and cut-off thought breeds a series of energy chain reactions in your entire psychic system. The power of choosing which thought to think in itself stems from strong energy movements and results in affect. Therefore consciousness must be one with energy.

In the average human state this does not seem to hold true, at first sight. However, when you go deeper, you are bound to see that whatever knowledge you harbor has a definite feeling content. As I said — and I purposely repeat this, for it cannot be emphasized enough in this context — dry, cut-off knowledge must also contain feelings. The underlying feeling may be fear. The more superficial energetic state may be boredom. Boredom is also an energetic state, although a negative one — negative in the sense that the absence of something does not mean that what is absent is not intrinsically and essentially present. It is only temporarily made absent. If you pursue the state of boredom deeper into the recesses of the soul substance, you will find that there is always fear somewhere: fear of knowing all you can know now, about yourself and about your relationship with the universe.

The relationship between you and the universe becomes increasingly obvious as you discover yourself, as you become more honest with yourself, as you stop acting out. States of consciousness can roughly be differentiated into the following three states: slumber, self-awareness, and cosmic consciousness.

The State of Slumber

The first and least developed is the state of slumber, where a being does not know it exists. It has no self-awareness. It can feel and move and grow, and even, to an extent, think, but below the threshold of self-awareness, like a mineral or a plant. The organisms beneath the state of self-awareness have nevertheless built-in patterns of creation, self-creation, which a particular organism follows through in a deeply meaningful, purposeful way, always compatible with its particular lawfulness. These states are states of consciousness, but not states of self-consciousness. Take for example the life of a plant: It follows its own built-in plan. Only its now-slumbering consciousness could create that plan, could create the imprint with all its own lawful cycles by which the organism lives, expands, dies, reincorporates itself, gives birth to itself, expresses itself and goes on in that same cycle. This requires an immensely intelligent plan that only consciousness could fabricate. Something like this cannot happen "by itself," cannot be a dead, disconnected process.

The apparent disconnection of inanimate matter is only temporarily frozen consciousness. When consciousness creates in a certain direction, the life spark slows down and down, until the energetic stream petrifies. It condenses into such a thick crust that the underlying energy is invisible; that is, not visible to the human eye. However, beings whose expanded state of consciousness makes them capable of perceiving more than the surface, can observe very clearly the highly potent energy within inanimate matter which has no manifest consciousness. But such beings can also perceive the consciousness content within this potent energy, the consciousness contained within the outwardly "dead" material.

What does such consciousness "say" when it is aslumber? It may say, "I do not want to know; I do not want to know me — me in relationship to the world around me." This statement is a creative nucleus —a statement made by consciousness, by deliberate choice and disposition. This statement brings forth an inexorable chain of events, leading gradually but surely to the condensed, slowed-down state that finally becomes a "crust," hardened and apparently dead. This is what matter is composed of. The sequence of events leading to the state of hardened, inanimate matter stems from a negative, life-and truth-negating statement. Nevertheless, once the hardening process is in action, matter itself can be used by consciousness for life-affirming and positive purposes. Free consciousness can thus "communicate" with the life-substance and consciousness within the hardened matter.

I give you this very brief explanation so that you can gain some concept about the fact that consciousness exists even within inanimate objects. Your scientists today have already ascertained that energy exists within matter, so that part is hardly news to you. You have yet to ascertain that the same holds true about consciousness.

Consciousness within inanimate objects is reachable by the much stronger and more active consciousness of the human mind, though to a lesser degree than the consciousness within plants, animals, or other human beings. Matter is still malleable and can be impressed by human consciousness. Since consciousness is capable of inventing and creating, it can mold, shape, and form out of the substances within matter. Take, for example, the need to produce a piece of furniture, or a plate, or a glass, or a piece of jewelry, or whatever the inanimate object may be. That need —that desire to create these objects —molds the energy, and contained consciousness, like inanimate matter, receives the imprints of a directing, stronger, and more connected consciousness, and fuses with it in certain definite ways. Thus an object is created.

So every object you use, enjoy, or need fulfills its task. Its innermost nucleus of consciousness that always seeks expression toward the divine, toward service, toward truth, toward love, toward being even in this separated deadened state "replies" to the creation of mind and thus fulfills a purpose in the great plan of evolution. Even the deadest of all dead matter is not really dead. Spiritual beings, who are in greater possession of their innate divine faculties and not bound to the purely outer manifestation as human beings are, can perceive the energy form and the consciousness expression of the most inanimate objects. Such an object also contains an energy field, which is its antenna, its receiving station, so that it must become a reactor. Its consciousness content is still too limited to be more than a reactor. It cannot be as yet an initiator and creator as the human state is, but it is definitely a reactor.

You may often find that you have certain relationships with objects. There are some objects you cherish, need and enjoy. They perform well for you. You may think that you love them because they perform well and give you good service, or beauty, or joy. But it is one of those benign circles working where it is hard to say what or who started it going. Take, for example, a motor car, or a machine you use, like a record player, or whatever it may be. You love that machine. You may even use it for your spiritual growth in one manner or another, so the purely utilitarian object is really not so utilitarian after all. You give it care. Your appreciation makes the machine respond, even with its extremely limited, small inner nucleus of consciousness that is just geared to respond and react, to be impressed and molded. Its energy field will be affected. With other objects it is the other way round. They never work out well. You hate them, are annoyed with them, and they respond accordingly.

The separation of consciousness that you experience is therefore a very debatable one. When we speak of the fact that the whole universe is permeated with consciousness, this is indeed a truth. Separated organisms, objects and entities are separated only on the surface level. But within and beneath that surface level there is a constant interaction.

I started to speak about the three stages of consciousness. I dwelled for a long time on the first state: consciousness without self-awareness. Animals, plants, minerals, and inanimate matter fall under this category. I wanted to show that nothing exists that does not contain consciousness. It is of course much easier to see this with animals and plants which have their growth and change processes.

The State of Self-Awareness

The second state is self-awareness, which begins at the human level. What does self-awareness mean? Awareness of "I am," "I exist," "I can think," "I can make a decision," "My decisions have impact," "My thoughts have effect," "My feelings reach other beings." This will be roughly the second state. In this state self-responsibility begins. The awareness of having an effect on the world around the self must result in accountability and the seriousness of choosing thoughts, attitudes, actions and responses. This state of consciousness, by virtue of its expanded awareness, finds many new alternatives which are lacking in the blind and more limited state. The state of consciousness below the threshold of self-awareness cannot make choices. It blindly follows the built-in pattern implanted in its substance. The human state is capable of re-creating the plan, and may increasingly avail itself of wider possibilities of self-expression commensurate with its own growth.

It is obvious that within the human state of consciousness, of self-awareness, there are many, many degrees and variations. Some human beings are as yet unaware of themselves, of their power to create, change and affect. Their ability to differentiate is as yet limited; their power to think and act independently is equally limited. To them words such as these would be meaningless and could hardly make more sense than to an animal. There are other human beings whose consciousness is already far more developed. They know quite well that they have the power to choose, to create and to affect.   They are self-responsible and accountable for their decisions to think one way rather than another. To them such words make sense and are an inspiration and encouragement.   There are of course many degrees of consciousness between these two categories.

However, even those human beings whose consciousness is least developed are aware that they exist. They know that they have needs and can, up to a degree, figure out how to fulfill these needs. They know that they can act. Maybe their scope is more limited than the scope and power to affect of a more highly developed human personality, but nevertheless there is an immense difference between them and the most highly developed animal state of consciousness. The latter may have some awakening power of thinking, but self-consciousness, in the sense I have described, is completely lacking.

The human state of self-awareness lives within its self-created dimension of time. Thus the sense of past, present, and future awakens in the human mind, but does not exist in the lower states of consciousness.

As in many areas of development, there is a similarity between the lowest and the highest point of the curve, which in this case is the state of being. Inanimate matter, minerals, plants, and animals do not live within time. They exist in a timeless state of being, but they are without self-consciousness, self-determination, a self-propelling initiative. The human state of consciousness is in time. It is therefore not in the state of being, but in the state of becoming, though it is already fully in possession of self-awareness. On the highest rise of the curve we return to the timeless state of being, but with a high degree of consciousness.

Cosmic Consciousness

This third state is the highest state of the three. We might call it universal consciousness, or perhaps cosmic consciousness. In this state all is one, there is no separation. In this state of consciousness all is known. The innermost self is known, the God-self is known. The God-self of the personal entity, as well as that of other entities, is known. The truth of being is known. In this state of consciousness you live in a state of being. But on this level of development the state of being surpasses self-awareness. It has reached universal awareness. To put this differently, and possibly more accurately: The self is recognized as being in all that exists.

If you meditate about the deeper meaning of these three states, you will see a great deal and understand much more about the greater life of which you form a part. The "innocent" state of being can exist in purity only. This purity can exist in one who is still blindly unaware, unconscious, and powerless, or in one who has regained the state of innocence through the laborious descent and simultaneous ascent of self-purification. Then power can merge with the timeless state of the eternal now.

There is a self-protective lawfulness in the lack of awareness of the innate potency of consciousness as long as the soul is not purified. As you can all so clearly observe on your path, this power increases in exact proportion to your ability to be in truth with yourself and others.

However unjust an evil manifestation may now appear to you, it appears that way only because in your limited time-bound state you are not in possession of the connections. Were you thus aware, you would see that all negative manifestations, no matter how cruel or unjust they may seem, are self-created medicine for the purpose of ultimate purification and ultimate bliss. Evil does not and cannot destroy — it can do so only temporarily and within the framework of what I just mentioned. If consciousness could expand without the simultaneous expansion of the self-purifying agents, evil could destroy the divine. So, as a built-in protective mechanism, negativity closes the perceptive organs: Blindness, deafness, dumbness, and numbness set in. The only way to come out of this state of ignorance, limitation, powerlessness, of being severed from the nucleus where there is all-connecting life, is by the constant attempt to know yourself where you are now —not to know the universe or anything outside you. That comes later—gratuitously, as it were. To concentrate on that would be pursuing a delusion.

Knowing yourself is a slow, step-by-step process. It doesn't ever require an impossible feat of you. It demands only what is indeed possible, to deal with something right there in front of your eyes, if you only choose to see it. You can use your best will and intent to find out what you ought to know about yourself at every step of the way. There is no fraction of time in your life, my friends, where this is not possible. You can be sure that when you are in a disharmonious state, you are not as aware as you could be. To become more aware often requires intense groping and searching. And that is indeed part of your life task. You may often look in the wrong direction for the answer to the present disharmony. Indeed, you often resist because you fear something much worse than what actually exists. You would find this out if only you had the courage and determination to go all the way, at all times.

The disharmonious state, the anxious state, the unhappy state, the depressed state, the state of unrest and fear and negative, contracted pain is always a reflection of something you might know right now, but choose —yes, literally choose —not to know. That choice creates a very potent negative energy field. This path helps you to deactivate these negative energy fields by changing the consciousness content in them. The first vital step here would be to transform the "I do not want to know" into an "I want to know," and follow it through. You can give yourself this adventure of discovery.

In the preliminary stages of this phase of evolutionary development, you must eliminate the blind spots about the self, so that the self can find out the answers about itself. You cannot awaken into a higher state as long as you do not know what you choose, what you think, what you feel, what you need, what you desire. Once you do know, you have increased your power to change what is destructive and undesirable.

As you go on in this way, there will come a period in which you know yourself fairly well, but you are not yet fully aware of others. Thus you grope with the manifestation of others. In your blindness to another person's negativity, or its exact nature, you may often lose yourself in confusion and disturbance. Further honest work will lead you to a clear awareness of others. This will bring you peace and show the way to deal with situations. Along the way, you will discover new aspects, often very positive ones, about yourself. Often only a crisis with others can bring forth such previously ignored aspects.

Self, Others, Universe

The first phase, as we have seen, is purely self-explorative. The second phase —often overlapping with the first —expands into knowledge of others. The third phase leads to universal knowledge beyond the human state. That is the organic development of this path. When I say knowledge, my friends, remember that there are different ways of interpreting this word. You may have knowledge on a purely mechanical level. Such knowledge is not insight, wisdom, true perception. It does not give you a sense of wonder and awe, nor does it fill you with peace and joy. It is dry, cut-off knowledge. I am talking about a different kind of knowledge, in which a kind of comprehension takes place that unites fragmented understanding. It is a deep and feeling knowledge that indeed brings peace and joy, awe and excitement. A revelation fills you that removes all dissension. You experience and relate in a new way. But this comes only much later on the path, my friends. At first you will experience the beginnings of this kind of knowledge only occasionally.

The more you expand, the more this kind of knowledge will fill you. And as that goes on, little by little, cosmic knowledge occurs. It comes from something deep within you. It transcends the personal. It is timeless and it gives you a deep awareness of the ongoing, ever-present life that you *are* and that everything *is*. This fills you with indescribable joy, peace, security, and gratitude for what exists. You must earn this awareness, my friends, for you cannot aim directly at cosmic consciousness. It is the final state of expanded self-awareness that you cultivate on a path such as this.

What I told you in this lecture is specifically designed to make you aware of the potency of your thoughts, of the potency of each thought that you decide to think, each attitude you decide to adopt. Thought will create experiences and responses, and will also create within you. There it will either create a new energy field or it will enforce, reaffirm and fasten an old one, depending on whether the thought or intent is new or is a repetition of the old. Obviously, both alternatives can apply to either real or false, constructive or destructive energy fields. When you are truly conscious of this potency, you become more responsible and more capable of creating. You then approach the state in which you know that God-consciousness

is within everything. The ego decides only which way to turn.
Right now, within your thinking mind is the potential to
express God's consciousness any way you choose. And when
your experience is negative, make sure to find out what created
it and how it was created.

You can all discover the truth of the power of your consciousness by making the commitment now, again and again, to
be in truth with yourself in your daily concerns, in your reactions, in experiences that leave you puzzled, confused or disturbed. When you feel resistance, admit the resistance, rather
than glossing over it, as you may be tempted to do. Have faith
in the truth. More and more, you will become free and joyous
and will liberate yourself of the shackles that now still keep you
confined in a state less than your birthright. Make the commitment to truth in every possible situation, about any conceivable incident.

With this message and suggestion I bless you all with deep
love —the love of the universe —for all of you, my most beloved
friends. Be in peace.

Part Five

Time: Pre-Birth and Post-Birth

"Time isn't holding us;
Time isn't after us."
— *David Byrne and Talking Heads*

The Pathwork lectures offer ideas and insights that are truly mind-stretching, while also generously assuming that our wiser, deeper selves are perfectly capable of understanding even the most radical spiritual truths. The topic of time is one particularly compelling subject addressed: what it is, on earth and in the spirit realm, and how our experience of time in our lives relates to our task of transformation.

We human beings seem to be continually trying to escape from the present moment by pushing forward into the future or pulling back into the past. The first lecture invites us to fully utilize every fragment of time available to us, and relentlessly demonstrates the consequences if we don't. Any feelings of impatience, listlessness, resentment, hostility and many other negative emotions can be traced directly to our not using time correctly. Ultimately, our restless pushing and pulling can be traced to our repressed fear of death. When we face this in ourselves, and fearlessly use every moment as an opportunity for self-examination and growth, we become alive and joyous, able to fully harmonize with and celebrate the present.

As we began this incarnation, we came into life in a state of forgetting — with all memory of our timeless past blotted out. It is usually only much later in life that some of us begin to remember who we really are, and what is our true purpose for being here on earth. This pre-birth amnesia serves a profound purpose, allowing as-yet-unpurified parts of ourselves to emerge, to offer themselves to be transformed. This lecture reveals why this self-purification couldn't happen any other way, and how our birth into a state of amnesia actually serves to aid our spiritual evolution.

D.T.

CHAPTER 12

Humanity's Relationship to Time

Greetings, my dearest, dearest friends. Blessings for every one of you. Blessings for your work on this path.

May you all be flooded by a wave of hope and security that you live in a benign universe in which you have nothing to fear.

I will now discuss a new topic: humanity's relationship to time. What I will say may at first seem utterly inapplicable to your personal lives because of its abstract nature. But if you have patience, and try to follow the deeper meaning of my words, you will soon see that they do have a very practical application.

Human existence on earth is bound by time. Time is a creation of the mind. Without the mind, time does not exist. In your dimension time, space, and movement are three separate elements of reality. When humanity reaches a higher degree of consciousness and with it an extended dimension, time, space, and movement begin to integrate more and more, until they become one. However, it is an error to believe that the next higher dimension is timelessness. There are many extended "times," if I may use this expression, in the higher realms of being, long before you reach the state of being that is timeless. As yet it is impossible for humanity to fully grasp this. The best you can do is to sense this truth occasionally.

The Limits of Time

Time is a very limiting existential modality. It is a fragment, cut from a wider and freer dimension of experience. The limited fragment, called time, is at the disposal of human beings so that they can grow, fulfill themselves, experience and reach happiness and liberation up to the limit commensurate with this dimension. To the degree that they fulfill their potential through inner growth, their life will be a dynamic and full experience within which the limitation of time will not be a hardship.

At this point, because it has so much bearing on this topic, I should like to interject once again that it is possible to be on a path of self-development on the whole and nevertheless miss many an opportunity for growth. How many times does it happen that you find yourself in a negative mood without learning the deep lesson behind it or seeing its significance for your innermost being? Instead, you simply wait for the mood to pass by itself. In these instances you do not utilize time well and it becomes a burden and a source of conflict. If you use each such growth opportunity for going to the root of the negative incident or mood, you will experience deep understanding and liberation. Then the exhilaration and trust in life and in yourself that you now experience only occasionally will become a more permanent state. Then you will be at one with the time element of your dimension, thereby organically growing into an extended time dimension.

Listlessness, depression, impatience, nervousness, anxiety, tension, frustration, boredom, apathy, and hostility —all these emotions and many others are in the last analysis a result of unutilized time. If you don't do the utmost possible to understand yourself and dissolve inner conflict and confusion, you cannot avoid the negative emotions that are unleashed when time goes by unutilized.

To those of my friends who have experienced liberation from such emotions with an influx of strength and inner joy, feeling that they are at one with life, I say: You can repeat this experience whenever you do not shirk the effort of looking deep into yourselves until you discover the origin of all the negative emotions. As you recall these times of liberation, you know that they were always connected with such efforts on your part. And to those of you who have not, as yet, had this experience, because you may be too new on this path, I say: It can be yours if you do what is necessary.

The vague knowledge that the time at your disposal is limited in this earth-dimension creates a special tension. You therefore strive to get out of this limitation of "time," straining as a dog pulls at its leash. Time holds you in its grip and you feel imprisoned in a fragment of reality. The unconscious still has a memory of the great experience of timelessness and tries to find its way back into a limitless freedom. This can be done, but only by accepting and fully utilizing the fragment you call time. Then the transition into freedom will be an organic flow with a minimum of conflict. Or you can, of course, resist by straining against the transition and not utilizing time in the way I describe and all true spiritual teachers point out. Then, inevitably, conflicts and tensions arise.

Fleeing the Now

Let us now discuss the particular conflict that human beings have with time. Each one of you has the possibility of finding out the truth of what I say, provided you take the necessary steps of self-investigation. As I have already indicated, human beings strive to reach a freer dimension of time. Translated into practical life, this manifests by striving toward tomorrow. If you observe yourself closely from this particular viewpoint, you will find it to be true in so many instances. Sometimes this is quite obvious because your thoughts are on the surface; at other times it permeates you as a vague general climate and is therefore not easily recognizable.

People strive toward the future mainly for two reasons: You do not like the present and hope for something better from the future; or else you fear a certain aspect of life and want to leave it behind in the past. Your vague hopes for the future and the unpleasant, unfulfilled state of the present are your reasons for straining away from the present and into the future. Thus you avoid living in the now. If, however, you were to explore within yourself the reasons for your unfulfillment and the difficulties which cause you to strain away from them, you would be capable of living in the now fully, meaningfully, and dynamically, deriving all the many joys from each moment that you now overlook. If each moment were truly lived to its fullest, you would already reach an extended dimension of time, while still remaining in this earth-dimension. The truth is that only by fully utilizing the dimension you live in can you outgrow it. Experiencing everything that each moment of time contains will stop you from straining away; you will thereby automatically find yourself flowing into the next time-dimension.

As always, awareness is the first step. So, do become aware of your inner striving away from the now. You will then find that you struggle against the now because you have not really found and resolved the causes that make you strain into the future.

The picture is entirely the opposite on the other end of the conflict. Human beings fear the future while they strive forward into it, because the future also means death and decay.

While they strain into the future, hoping for fulfillment, they simultaneously try to stem the tide of time, desiring to stop its movement, or even go backward into youth. People want two impossible things: the fulfillment of the future in the past or, at least, in the present. This wish generates two contradictory soul movements: One strains forward, the other holds back. Needless to say, the soul suffers from tension, a useless and destructive waste of energy.

Some time ago I discussed the fear of death, which is an integral part of the conflict with time. Fear of death causes a backward movement opposed to the natural movement of time which is a steady, harmonious flow. If you can feel into its rhythm, you will be in harmony. You can do so by being in time in the only meaningful way, using each moment and incident for growth. Not straining away from the future, you will not have to fear it. Not pulling away from the present, you will utilize it well, so that it will not seem desirable to strain away from it. This is *being,* even if it is not yet the highest state of being. It is the state of being commensurate with the dimension of time you live in.

Following the Wave of Time

Once in this state, you follow the natural flow. The wave of time will bring you naturally and gracefully into the next extended dimension, which you fear so much because you cannot yet prove its reality. Your very haste to get into the new dimension, on the one hand, and your fear of the unknown, on the other, are reactions to what seems so uncertain to a part of your personality. With these reactions you restrain the natural movement and create tension, setting your soul forces to work in opposing directions. The result is stagnation of growth, as well as lack of the full experience of each "now."

After you determine the subtle but nevertheless very distinct inner double motion, you will find a psychological value in understanding the nature of the emotions and attitudes responsible for the contradictory soul movements.

The *daily review*[6] I advocate is one of the best means toward living each day and each hour fully. I venture to say that all my friends who work so diligently on this path have, at least occa-

---

6. See Glossary for definition of **daily review**.

sionally, experienced the special peace that is full of the spark of aliveness, as dynamic as it is peaceful, after having recognized in all its depth a distortion or a negative attitude in themselves. If all the benefit contained in the recognition has been derived from it, then this wonderful feeling of aliveness is bound to manifest.

That the recognition itself may be very unflattering and dis-illusioning about oneself, and at times even painful, will not diminish the great experience once the recognition is complete. On the contrary. This may furnish the best proof of the truth of my words. Also, you may use the peaceful experience as a yardstick. Whenever a self-confrontation does not, in the end, produce an uplifting experience, you have not found all that is to be discovered.

Have you ever thought, my friends, why it is that, after an unflattering or painful recognition —provided you go to its very depth and do not stop halfway —you experience such a dynam-ic state of harmony and aliveness? It is so only because, at that moment, you have fully utilized what is given to you, the frag-ment of time at your disposal. When you are listless and depressed, or in any way unhappy, the material is there, right in front of you; you are right in it, but you are blind to it. You do not focus your attention on it. You merely try to get out of this "now" without utilizing it. That is the forward movement which also causes your fear of growing into death —which is actually a threshold of life. Therefore you hold back while you also push forward.

Fear of death exists in many forms and shapes. Any spiritu-al or religious belief, if it is superimposed from the outside and not experienced inwardly, is as much a part of the fear of death as a violent protestation of unbelief. They are but two different sides of the same coin.

The only way to experience the flow of time that knows no interruption, that brings you into extended dimensions, is to utilize each living moment in the manner you learn on this path. Then you no longer deal with concepts which you adopt or reject, which you agree or disagree with. An inner experience comes into being that makes you realize that the present matrix of time is only one facet of another matrix of time; it is but a fragment of a bigger piece. This, in itself, brings the knowledge that death is but an illusion. Death is merely a manifestation of transition into a different dimension. However, such words can be meaningful only if you make the experience of their reality possible.

Are there any questions now pertaining to this topic?

QUESTION: You say that once one leaves this dimension of time one enters another time which involves unification of space, time, and movement. Will you please clarify that?

ANSWER: Yes, I will try. In your dimension, time and space are two separate factors. I give you a practical example: You find yourself in a certain space, you require time to get there. In order to bridge the distance, movement is necessary. So, movement is the bridge that combines time and space. In the next dimension, where there is a wider fragment of what you may call time —which is still far from timelessness — movement, time, and space are one. In other words: You are in one space. You think of the space you wish to be in. The movement required to bridge the distance is your thought. It is of a shorter span of time and motion. Thought, which is movement, brings you into another area of space, regardless of the distance, as measured in your dimension. Do you understand that?

QUESTION: Yes. But it brings two questions to mind. One is: Can this happen on earth? And two: I saw a TV program recently which explained that in outer space, as we know it today, this adjustment via movement through time and space takes place, so that the time changes according to the rate of speed you are traveling in space. I don't quite understand it.

ANSWER: To bridge distance with thought is not possible on earth with material means. The spirit, the psyche, is, of course, capable of experiencing this. In fact, it experiences it constantly, but the waking brain is rarely aware of it. The physical body is incapable of the experience because it is made and adjusted to the limited dimension in which a separation between time and space exists, and the bridge between these is movement.

As to your second question: When material and technical means have been invented to leave this dimension, an inkling of this factor becomes accessible to material brain knowledge. But whether or not the discovery is understood in its more profound meaning depends, of course, on the individual—on the capacity and willingness of people to understand. I might add that the technical knowledge that brought this cosmic truth into your material world — the same truth that I approached here from a different angle —is a consequence of a general, overall readiness of this earth-sphere to grasp higher truth.

If, in spite of the possibility for growth that brought such higher truth into its grasp, humanity still does not learn the deeper meaning from it, humanity will stagnate. It is exactly the same process with an individual. A person who has potential to grow but does not utilize it will be a more troubled soul than the one who may actually exert less effort in the direction of individual development but is closer to the given potential. This explains why it is impossible to judge and compare.

To get back to your question: The technical discoveries are one way of helping humanity to acquire a broader awareness. But if a technical discovery does not lead to broader and deeper understanding, such discovery will not only be useless, it will turn destructive. The constructiveness and benefit of every discovery depends on whether or not humanity as a whole understands spiritual and cosmic law on a deeper level than it did before such a discovery was made. If this happens, it will help humanity to produce greater inner freedom, faster growth and development, and therefore outer peace and justice in increased measure.

If history is observed from this point of view, it will be found that every upheaval that humanity has experienced on earth is a result of broader knowledge used without the proper understanding. The links between new knowledge in certain eras and the subsequent upheavals due to ignorance of the real meaning of the knowledge could be established if historians undertaking such a search were, themselves, in a fully growing life-process. New knowledge is not necessarily and exclusively of a technical nature. It can be an influx in art, philosophy, or any realm of experience. The links are not immediately visible, but they are there. It might be an interesting study for a historian who has the inner equipment to see that which first seems obscure, but which stands out clearly once one's attention is focused in the right direction.

What you mentioned in your second question is the same in technical terms as what I explained in philosophical and psychological terms.

My dearest friends, be blessed again, every one of you. May these words not merely pass through your brain. May they, indeed, give you the incentive to listen deeply within yourself in order to gain a little distance from yourself. Just by gaining more objectivity, you may become more at home with yourself and feel more at ease with life in this fragment of time, so that you may utilize it fearlessly, neither straining toward the future nor stemming against it.   Therefore you will be in harmony with the flow of time.   Thus, gradually, through the discoveries about your innermost hidden attitudes and emotions, you will find yourself flowing with the wave of time, in harmony with it, living each now to the fullest.   May all of my good friends— those who are present and those who are absent, those who are new and those who are hesitant, those who may contemplate to begin a new way of inner life —may you all find your real self and thus eventually overcome the barrier that makes you tend to the visible manifestation, while being blind to what causes it.

Be in peace.   May you find the strength and the reality that I try to help you find.   Be blessed.   Be in God!

Reawakening From Pre-Incarnatory Anesthesia

Greetings. Loving blessings are pouring forth for every one of you.

In this lecture, I will again speak about the phenomenon of consciousness, particularly in connection with the evolutionary process and the meaning of individual life.

All knowledge is in you. I have often said this, but it is rarely understood. Before you are born into this life, a process of anesthesia sets in. There is a specific reason for this. You awaken from it, as you come out of infancy, with a limited consciousness. The awakening is partial and gradual. As you grow physically, mentally, and emotionally, you grope to rediscover your inner knowledge. At first you do this in a limited way, with a focus on material life. You learn to walk, handle objects, you speak; you learn reading, writing, numbers, certain basic laws of outer life, of physical matter that surrounds you and that you will need to handle.

Once basic material knowledge is mastered or reawakened, deeper knowledge is reacquired, provided that the growth process takes place as planned. When a person is in an intensive growing process, this will happen in ever-increasing depth and scope. If the person has stopped the movement of the growth process — his "life train"— that interruption will prevent the reacquisition of knowledge he or she possesses in a potential state.

The Reason for Anesthesia

Here you will inevitably have to ask, "Why does anesthesia set in?" Actually, the anesthesia sets in well before the birth process. In your spiritual reality, where the total entity that you *are* truly belongs, you decide upon a reappearance in this dimension. That is when you are deliberately anesthetized.

After all plans for your life on the material plane are thoroughly discussed and assimilated, you lose consciousness. A person who undergoes an operation goes through a similar process. In fact the process of anesthetization is copied from the spirit life, remembered and rediscovered in earthly life. On earth its purpose is to prevent pain during an operation. In the case of the incarnatory process, the reason is different.

Before the spiritual self takes possession of the human body in the birth process, the entity is already in a sleeping state, anesthetized and unaware. At birth, there is an awakening to a slight degree —slight in relation to its actual state. The limited part of the entity that takes possession of the infant body finds itself awake to physical sensations and functioning, and to certain limited perception and awareness; none of these can be properly assessed, interpreted, or assimilated. That comes later. The state of awareness after birth is increased but is still very limited. Becoming aware and awake is a gradual process.

The first years —roughly, the first twenty-two to twenty-five years, although this cannot be generalized—are primarily focused on acquiring outer knowledge. Provided the process is meaningful and organic, the focus should then go to acquiring knowledge that transcends the physical reality: inner, spiritual knowledge. This can take place first on a psychological level. I include psychological knowledge when I speak of spiritual knowledge, for it concerns itself with the laws and processes of the inner self.

Certain highly developed individuals with a capacity for spiritual fulfillment often, though not always, awaken to inner reality earlier, which can coincide with the outer learning. This can happen because the knowledge is near and deeply anchored into the soul; in previous lifetimes it had become such an integral part of the entity that it is easier to reawaken than in others without such previous development, who must still go through processes of growing, searching, and struggling before the inner knowledge penetrates every particle of the soul. That is, of course, what life is all about. And all of it is necessary: The groping process, the process of trial and error, searching, often being confused and not knowing, dealing with the not-knowing in a constructive way. One must find the often precarious balance between patience and humility for the grace of knowledge to communicate itself on the one hand, and serious commitment, endeavor, focused will and healthy aggression on the other. This process is the key.

Now I return to the question of why the temporary anesthetizing takes place. I recapitulate briefly: The manifest personality does not know what it knows. Knowledge, to whatever degree it exists, is blotted out; it is "forgotten." Whatever state of development you may be in, you start off with a clean slate: You start off knowing nothing. The knowledge that is in you is, apparently, *not* in you. Now, why must that be?

In a lecture about the evolutionary process,* I discussed how the "mass" of consciousness spreads, filling the void. As it does so, particles of consciousness lose themselves. The essential divine consciousness, in its beauty, wisdom, and benign power, functions in a limited and distorted way. The isolated particles must seek to unite again with the forward-rushing, spreading movement of the divine state of life that inexorably fills the void. In this process the separated particles —which are individual entities —must find the way back on their own, by dint of reawakening the divine potentials always present, even in the most separated aspects.

Let me try to make this clear. Suppose you were consciously to know, now, all that you deeply know. Then the undeveloped aspects in you would not find, under their own steam, their innate essence. They would be swept along, as it were, by the already-knowing, already-developed aspects. They would therefore always represent an unreliable element. They would essentially, although not necessarily manifestly, blur the beauty, vitality, creativity, and wisdom of the rest of your being. They would be carried by the surge of the glory of God-consciousness, but they would not be totally infused with it. Purification and evolution mean that every smallest aspect of all that is must be infused with its own essence.

Let us apply this somewhat metaphysical and general explanation to your present state, your everyday life and struggle on your path. You may then not only understand better what I am saying, but will personally benefit from it.

The Worst Needs to Emerge

On your path you constantly discover aspects of negativity, irrationality, childishness, selfishness, and destructiveness. You know that these aspects flare up, at an early stage of your development, by themselves, without provocation from out-

---

* Pathwork Guide Lecture # 218.

side. These aspects are so strong that you activate them, initiating negativity, regardless of what the outer situation is. As your development proceeds, this changes. The negative aspects cease to manifest by themselves. They need outer provocation. You respond with them to the initiating negativity of others around you. However, you do live in the world of matter, in which, under even the best of circumstances, life is not easy. Matter obstructs and frustrates. The very fact of living in this dimension of reality —which is your production, of course —is always a challenge. Imagine that you lived under circumstances so sublime, favorable and bliss-producing, that even the worst in you would not find occasion to express itself. Then the worst in you would remain dormant, unexposed, and would not go through its necessary process of purification.

You are often convinced, and partially rightly so, that if others did not do this or that, you would be fine, you would stay in a state of harmony and bliss. The blurred areas in you would, however, continue to smolder, because without their manifestation you would not know of their existence. They need exactly to be triggered, they need the exposure and provocation. By the same token, if you were consciously to know all you know, with no provocations from outside, the undeveloped aspects would not flare up and would not acquire their own ingrained knowing. They would merely be affected by what the already developed aspects know.

On your path you have experienced that when you successfully work through those blurred areas, you become absolutely safe, no matter what others do or fail to do, no matter how they react. You remain essentially whole, essentially unaffected. I do not mean unaffected in the sense of being remote and without feeling. I mean that the particular negativity in you that you have worked through no longer exists and therefore cannot flare up when others do wrong by you. You may be hurt or angry, but in an entirely different way than when your own unresolved faults and flaws are triggered by outside circumstances. *So you no longer depend on perfection in order not to face your imperfection.* The effect of others' destructiveness will not make you lose your bearing or your center if your blurred areas have been clarified, purified, cleansed, and eliminated.

The same principle holds in the relationship between your own inner imperfections and your already purified parts. If you were born knowing all you know, the uncleansed areas would depend on the cleansed ones and not become whole within themselves. If the wise, knowing, enlightened aspects of your-self are asleep, that sleep is necessary to allow the blurred areas to struggle through on their own, with the aid of the knowledge that is essentially in you. Thus out of a lack of knowledge, knowledge is developed. Out of the darkness light develops. Even in the darkest, most ignorant part is the essence of knowl-edge and light. That essence must express from within itself, not from an aspect outside itself already in possession of wis-dom and light. So when the knowledge and light are brought forth from within your own limitations, purification is thor-ough, reliable and real. Then true independence from one's sur-roundings is being established and thus, true freedom. Then each particle, each aspect of consciousness has brought forth its own "minuscule Godness," so to speak. And that is the mean-ing of the anesthesia with which you enter into life. It is your struggle for your essential light that gradually and surely dimin-ishes the anesthesia and awakens you to who you really are.

Wisdom and Clarity Emerge

You also experience on your path that the more courage you muster to face your truth, the more humility and honesty you bring to bear on your whole inner person, the more alert and awake you become. This is an inexorable consequence that can-not fail to manifest. Suddenly, or gradually, you understand and perceive others in a way you never could before. You begin to recognize others' negativities without being personally affect-ed or disturbed by them. You no longer struggle against others' negativity in a blind, resentful way, without seeing clearly, only vaguely perceiving as through a fog. Now you see clearly; you comprehend intuitively the connections that make the trans-gression no longer a personal annihilation. You also begin to perceive others' beauty in a way that doesn't make you jealous but that fills you with awe, wonder, and gratitude. As you go on in that way, dealing with your own impurities and eliminat-ing them, a new focusing and awareness awaken inside of you. A knowledge flows into you, apparently from out of nowhere. It is not from the brain. It is not from the outer knowledge you have acquired in the first two decades of your life, or later. It comes from a different source.

As channels open, a new focusing can set in. You can begin very deliberately to listen into the inner universe, the place from which all wisdom flows into your outer being. It is a grad-ual process, yet it can be sudden in its manifestation. The process sometimes seems to be interrupted, because it often disappears at the initial stages, so that the experience can appear to have been a dream. The state in which you hear the inner voice must be fought for in a positive, relaxed sense. It must be gained and regained, for it is lost over and over again.

The focusing must be done quite deliberately after a certain stage of development and purification has been reached. The focusing will yield to connections, to listening and "hearing." Now, the state of consciousness in humanity as a whole, because of mass conditioning, makes such focusing virtually impossible. Many of those who are developed enough and could succeed don't even try. Their still unresolved problem may be fear of ridicule and disapproval from the world around them; they lack courage to establish the inner self as the true center of individual life. The whole of humanity is conditioned to focus only on certain phenomena, outside and inside, at the exclusion of other aspects of reality, until only that which is in their focus seems real. A whole world exists around you which you do not see or experience; it seems like a fantasy when you hear it discussed. This limitation of perception is the result of a conditioned reflex in focusing, which, in turn, is the result of anesthesia.

At the beginning of such a path, if you listen into yourself, you probably hear nothing and may become convinced that there is nothing but emptiness. Or perhaps you hear occasionally the voice of the childish, demanding, negative self. Then, of course, you are convinced that this is your final reality, which frightens you, and so you avoid facing the negative self even more until later when, perhaps, you learn to make room to listen deeper and are able to contact levels of unimagined inner reality.

Question and challenge your negative voice. Confront it. Identify it without being identified with it. Learn not to allow it to control you, not to act it out — even as you acknowledge the existence of this voice of selfishness and meanness. Only as this attitude becomes consistent, as confrontation between the lower self and the conscious, reasonable, positive ego-self takes place constantly, will you eventually find your focus on another level of consciousness which, as you will suddenly discover, has always been there.

The Voices of God and the Lower Self

The voice of God has always spoken to you. It continues to speak to you always in a new way, always adapted exactly to what you need most at any given moment in your life. It is the voice that you overlooked and kept out of focus so that you were left with the illusion of silence.

It is impossible to refocus on this beautiful voice by skipping over the confrontation with the lower self that also always speaks to you. Your ego has to learn to distinguish between them. The voice of the lower self says, "I want it for me. I do not care about others." That part of you believes in a mutual exclusivity, in a division of interests between you and others, and that it must triumph at the expense of others. That negative voice must be confronted, it must be questioned. Question the voices of meanness and malice, your stake in seeing others as bad, and not wishing to make room to even doubt this. Simultaneously see that you —or a part of you—doubt the beauty and trustworthiness of the universe. Question the voice of fear, question its lack of faith, and confront it sincerely. Then the ongoing voice of God will be heard. And you will recognize it. You will rediscover that it has always spoken to you, clearly and beautifully. You simply could not hear it before, because it could not push itself through as long as you deliberately focused away from it.

Focusing is deliberate, both in a positive and in a negative sense. In a positive sense, you had to be born in anesthesia, having forgotten what you know, to purify totally all aspects of the self. Had you always heard the divine voice, purification could not have taken place. You would not have been able to focus on the negative, or deal with it. It would have been quieted down and swept along. In a sense, focusing away from the divine voice is the anesthesia that your self deliberately chooses for the incarnatory process. In the negative sense, deliberate focusing away from the divine voice is due to the power you give to the negative self that rejects any rule but its own. The negative self does not want to know itself. Yet the divine voice leads the negative self to know itself. That is the first step for the negative self to purify itself.

Many of my friends on this path can perhaps begin to take deliberate steps toward hearing both voices distinctly. What is the negative, lower self? It may manifest under a clever disguise. And what is the divine voice? You can learn to deliberately shift your focus, and you can spend time in your meditation practicing this differentiation.

Now, my dearest friends, I bless all of you. Divine love and wisdom are here in abundance. You who work on this path create so much blessing for yourself, so much light. More and more you will awaken from your sleep, so that you will never have to fall asleep again. Rest will not impair the awareness of a joyous, peaceful, exciting, blissful universe in which you live and which lives in you. You are blessed.

Part Six

Specialists, Devils, and the Essence of Evil

"Everything praises God.
Darkness, privations, defects, evil too
praise God and bless God."
— *Meister Eckhart*

A spirit is a consciousness which does not dwell in a material body.

At all times and in all places and in all cultures, other than Western civilization of the last three hundred years, the existence of spirits has been known by all. The Torah of Judaism, the Old and New Testaments of Christianity, the Koran of Islam, all describe the actions of angels and devils, as they come to earth and play a role alongside men and women. Buddhists make offerings of food and prayers to the hungry ghosts; Confucianists say prayers to the spirits of ancestors; the ancient Greeks went to oracles with the expectation that a spirit voice would answer their questions. Every indigenous culture studied by anthropologists routinely interacts with the spirit realm through its myths and rituals.

It is only in the cultures of Europe and America, in the past few hundred years, that angels and devils have come to be viewed as superstitions which do not "really" exist. And therefore, most people have ceased to see them.

Recently, however, some people have begun to notice them again. This is irritating and threatening to the rationalists who believe only in physical reality and who must consider this to be a sort of backsliding to a more primitive time. However, it is clear to others that this is not a regression to superstition, but rather an emergence of heightened sensitivity and the sign of a further evolutionary development in human beings.

As many of us are evolving the capability to reach a state of cosmic consciousness, so are we becoming more able to perceive what has heretofore escaped the notice of our physical senses.

The Pathwork lectures take for granted the existence of a spiritual reality, and they describe its nature and many of its principles. I felt that what the lectures say about *negative spirits* and how they affect humanity is of great importance, and I feature that information in this section.

The world of spirit is more specialized than our world. The first lecture here explores the role of negative specialists, those spirits that attach to our faults and magnify and direct them. For our own protection we must face our faults honestly and commit to transforming them.

The second lecture in this section, on evil and consciousness, makes it clear that in the ultimate reality of the unified state there is no evil. At the same time, on the level of human manifestation, there is. An important part of our work is accepting this reality and facing and overcoming the evil that exists within us.

The third lecture specifically describes three principles of evil —separation, materialism and confusion — and how they arise and interact with one another.

D.T.

CHAPTER 14

Influence Between the Spiritual and Material Worlds

I bring you blessings and love, my friends.

I will speak about the influence between the spiritual and material worlds. Much has been said about the influence of the world of spirit on the world of matter, but not as much about the influence the other way around. For both affect each other.

First I will discuss the influence of spirit on your earthly sphere. There are spiritual spheres throughout the universe. Since distance in the world of spirit is not measured by your geographical measurements, it is possible for many spheres to exist on the same geographical or material spot and to overlap. For example, one human can live on earth, be in this room, and also be connected to a particular spiritual sphere, while another person in the same room can be connected to another sphere of quite a different level. I realize, my friends, this is extremely difficult for you to imagine, because distance for you is a question of space. Yet in absolute reality it is not so. A person is in contact with a sphere that corresponds to his or her general, overall spiritual development. Since no one on earth is harmoniously developed —if you were, you would not have to live here —you may at one time be in contact with a particular spiritual sphere, and when your mood changes, the currents coming out of your soul, your subconscious, and your conscious mind, will connect you with quite a different sphere.

I have explained to you about *the higher self, the lower self, and the mask self* [7]. Wherever the higher self has been restored to its original state by shedding the surrounding layers constituting

---

7. See Glossary for definition of **higher self**, **lower self**, and **mask self**.

the lower self, it reaches out and automatically connects with the highest and most radiant spheres, even though you still live on earth. And wherever the lower self is still stronger and does not permit the higher self to shine through, connection is made with the forces of darkness, according to each person's attitude and development. In other words, one person's lower self may be lower than another's. Since each sphere is richly populated by spirits fitting into that particular sphere, you are all constantly in touch with spirits of varying spiritual development, as well as with the forces and currents generating from our particular sphere.

Some people say that evil spirits are responsible when their lower self takes over, meaning that they are not to blame. But this is not true. Certainly, evil spirits can and do influence you, but only if and when you permit it by your laxity in pursuing your spiritual development and through your inclination to take the line of least resistance. You think that merely because your faults are not as bad as those of certain people of very low development —a criminal, for example — they do not matter so much. Even if your faults are only minor ones, not outright crimes or recognized sins, you are responsible. The higher your development, the more it is your responsibility and duty to perfect yourself. The more you are free of very wicked or evil trends, the higher your development evidently is. Therefore you possess more enlightenment and more strength and thus more can be expected of you. A so-called minor fault may count just as heavily for you as a crime would for a person of little or no spiritual enlightenment. Therefore, do not compare your faults and deviations from spiritual law with another's. Your comparison may be all wrong, because you cannot possibly judge where you stand compared to others. I am saying this because people often make allowances for themselves either by saying or thinking, "I am not the only one who does that; other people are doing worse," or by putting the blame on evil spirits whose influence on them, they like to believe, is merely arbitrary. By the same token, if higher entities from the world of God can guide, help, and influence you, it can be so only because your inner attitude has called them forth.

The Specialists

Wherever a human being is, a number of spirit beings of various stages of development are also close by. In every sphere there are specialists of all kinds. I have said this before and repeat it here because its significance is not yet fully understood. The world of spirit, in all its gradations, is much more specialized than your earthly sphere. This applies to the divine order and to the world of darkness as well as all the variations in between. Each one of you attracts those specialists whose particular qualities, good or bad, you possess. For like attracts like inevitably, magnetically. When a human being grows up, he or she is surrounded by guardian spirits who belong to the order and organization of divine worlds, and they can come close to their protégé only if he or she asks for divine truth and will, and tries to strive higher. Otherwise they have to stand back and watch from a distance. They will interfere only to protect according to past merits, following exact spiritual laws about which they are very careful and which they do not ever break, because these laws are perfection, love, wisdom and justice. This very same person is also surrounded by a number of other spirits not incorporated into the divine order. Some may belong to the world of darkness. If this person is not a criminal or a really sinful soul, very evil spirits will keep away, for they could not accomplish their specialty with such a person.

However, even the specialists of the so-called minor or everyday human faults belong to the world of darkness. They also operate according to their own laws and accomplish just as much for their purposes as, let us say, a spirit of murder who influences a human being. If your fault is selfishness, there will be a selfishness specialist attached to you. If your fault is that you are inclined to furious outbursts, you will have a specialist around you of a type who will wait for you to permit it to take over, influence you and thus live through you. This gives it a great deal of satisfaction, not only because it thus fulfills its task, but also because it can indulge in its particular weakness. On the other hand, you may be completely devoid of envy, so you do not have a specialist of envy attached to you. But another person not inferior to you in his or her overall development may have this envy specialist around because of this fault.

So you must bear in mind that it is your own faults that pull the particular specialists close to you in the first place, and that they constantly wait for an opportunity to live through you. Thus you collude with them, and can get rid of them only through your personal endeavor to overcome your faults. But before you can do this, you first have to recognize all your faults, of which you are often unaware simply because you do not want to be burdened with such unflattering knowledge. Few people really want to know their faults. Most people admit that they have some faults; but to admit faults in a superficial way and to become fully aware of them are two different things.

So, for your own protection, each one of you should face himself or herself in utter honesty. You can be sure that whatever your particular faults are, you will carry with you and around you the corresponding spirit specialists who are waiting for an opportunity to tempt you to give in to your particular faults. And since it does not take a lot of pressure to succumb, and it is the easy and comfortable way, very often you follow these temptations. The stronger the fault is within you and the less aware you are of its full significance, the closer this specialist will be to you! Thus it is at the same time both correct and incorrect for people who know about the existence of the beyond and the spirit-creatures to say that an evil spirit influenced them. When they say this, and mean by it that they are taking full responsibility for their own input, it is correct; but when they say it because they want to absolve themselves of personal responsibility and guilt, it is incorrect.

Between these low creatures and the higher entities of the world of God there are many spirits who are very similar to yourselves in their attitudes. They may be deceased people who mean well and are not particularly bad, but who do not yet belong to the divine order and are thus blind in many respects. They often seek to influence human beings because it helps them in some way, or simply because they have nothing better to do. They can learn from you if you take the spiritual path of self-development. However, if you are not stronger than they are, they will influence you, sometimes not harmfully; but, even though they may mean well, they do not inspire you to the best of your spiritual advantage because they are blind. Sometimes their guidance may be to your material advantage, which may or may not interfere with your spiritual progress; and sometimes their influence may be harmless or appear harmless, but is ultimately to your disadvantage. When and to what degree this can happen is again no coincidence: Their influence is inevitably called forth by your own inner attitudes.

If you meditate about this, about yourself, your life and your desires, you can find out what spirits are around you. Those of you who walk on the path of perfection, which is the only real protection you have, will not be bothered or influenced by spirits who do not fulfill the will of God in all respects. There are other means of protection, but they have only a temporary effect. If you are in disharmony — for instance when you feel a quarrel brewing with your fellow-creatures — and have the presence of mind to bring yourself to pray, to reach out for God within you, or to ask for spiritual guidance, this will surely help, and I recommend it strongly. But it will help only in this particular instance, since you do not always have such presence of mind. Sometimes you will be tired and will let yourself go, and then you become prey to these influences which, as we said, can have an effect on you only because of what is already within you. Therefore, the only definite and permanent cure and protection for you is to tear out the bad growths at their roots. This happens on the path of perfection and self-development, the path of happiness. If you are willing to take this path, you will be guided and helped. But first this will and decision must be clearly formulated within you; then it will be recognized. At that point your divine guidance can automatically and immediately get close to you and can, among other things, guide you to the proper human help which you also need in order to take this path. You will be guided to the place and the person best suited to your temperament and character.

This is how the different spiritual spheres with their respective creatures influence humans. Human beings are not helpless prey to these influences, but determine them. And by rejecting any influence that does not come from the divine world, a person not only takes hold of his or her own life but also weakens the forces of darkness, for the less they have to work with in the material world, the more power they must eventually lose.

Your Spiritual Creations

Humans have another kind of influence on the world of spirit. I will try to give you a picture of this, though it can only be a very limited one. You know that, as I have said many times, your thoughts and feelings are spiritual creations. They create forms of all kinds in the spiritual world. If your life is in accordance with your destiny, and you fulfill the maximum you are able to according to your development —which is very rarely the case —you create forms that will build harmonious spheres, structures, and landscapes in the spirit world. This may sound incredible to some of you. However, my dear ones, I assure you it is true! The day will come for all of you when you will see this truth. As a matter of fact, when you see it, you will know what you have known all along in spirit. This knowledge was only temporarily blurred from your consciousness while you were incarnated. People who give in to the lower self create forms that correspond to the quality, strength, and type of their lower self. This does not exclude their simultaneously creating harmonious and beautiful forms to the degree that their higher self is allowed to function.

Let us imagine that all humanity, meaning each individual, would follow the line of least resistance and give in to the lower self, and nurse it instead of fighting it. What would happen from our point of view? The overlapping spheres I have described would change in appearance. Humankind would strengthen and enlarge the disharmonious spheres, which would completely overcast the harmonious spheres of light, truth, love, and happiness, and push them into the background, so that they could affect humans less and less. As a result, only the influence of the disharmonious forces would have an effect. Humanity would thus constantly furnish material to the world of darkness, and its influence in turn would be that much greater on you. On the other hand, let us again imagine that all humankind —each individual person —would walk the path of perfection. This path would be different for each individual, because what may be necessary for one person may be much too difficult for another. Yet if all children of God, on whatever level of development, would try their best, the spheres of darkness and disharmony, evil and envy, hatred and prejudice, war and greed would be cast off and gradually dissolve. Divine creation, however, can never dissolve; it can only be pushed into the background so that it cannot affect the material world as long as the negative attitude remains in control there. Disharmony, with all its facets, can and must ultimately be destroyed and dissolved. So you can see very well not only how the spirit world affects you, but also how you affect it. A continuous cycle, whether vicious or benign, is set in motion between the two. This will never change as long as a material world exists; it must be this way.

For instance, if a group of human beings, perhaps only a very small group, comes together in the sincere and honest desire to serve God and His great plan, do you know what form we see in the spirit world? We see a very beautiful temple being built in the world of spirit. This group to which I manifest myself here is building such a temple, stone by stone. It is not completely erected, the roof is still missing, and it is not yet furnished, but the construction is well under way. Do not think that I speak symbolically; I am speaking the truth. This temple already exists in our corresponding spiritual sphere.

Former Incarnations

Are there any questions in connection with this, my friends?

QUESTION: I once wrote a play about a former incarnation in Egypt and I wonder if I myself was in Egypt in a former incarnation?

ANSWER: At this opportunity, may I give a short explanation to all my new friends here? Spirits belonging to the order of the divine plan cannot and will not give this kind of information unless it serves a very good purpose, unless it is important for self-development. If and when this information should become necessary for you, you will receive knowledge of it, either through me or through another spirit, or through enlightenment that will come directly to you. But as long as this is merely an interesting speculation, we do not give such information, because if we were to handle this so lightly, there would be no purpose for the memory to be taken away from one life to the next. I know there are many spirits coming through mediums who are very liberal with this kind of information. But they are not spirits of ours. It is easy to say, it satisfies human curiosity, and it can never be proven. A spirit could easily say to you "yes" or "no," and you would not know. You would be satisfied. But we do not do it that way. When such knowledge comes, it must have real meaning. It must be a key to your present life. Sometimes enlightenment is given on the subject of past lives. The country is rarely important, but other circumstances are important. Whenever truth pervades you about a previous incarnation —and this goes for all of you— you must have a feeling of victory, or liberation. It is as if a key were put into a keyhole and a door were opened, and all of a sudden you understand many, many things in your present life, such as difficulties, hardships, and tests. If that feeling does not accompany such information, do not trust it.

QUESTION: When, in the opinion of the spirit world, is a person initiated?

ANSWER: Well, since I am repeatedly asked this question,

I will try to answer it briefly; however, before I do that, I want to say this: The danger with human beings is that they use certain key words and labels very glibly and quickly. This is harmful. It would sometimes be better if you did not even know about these words. From our viewpoint, initiation takes place when a person has really, wholeheartedly, not only in thought and theory but in practice, given his or her life to God; when no other considerations matter at all; when God is always put first. This does not mean that you should become fanatics or go into a cloister. On the contrary. What is meant by complete surrender to God is that material comfort, the desires of the ego, become secondary to considerations pertaining to God and his great plan and the fulfillment of this life according to God's will. When this is recognized and a certain stage reached where this is consciously put into practice, then we might say that your word "initiation" could be applied.

QUESTION: Why is there an urge in man to search for spiritual life?

ANSWER: Because the higher self or the divine spark is in everyone, and it urges you in exactly this one direction. The lower the development, the more layers of the lower self cover the higher self, the more this urge is covered up. But when a certain development is reached, the wish of the higher self pushes you. And again some voices of your lower self try to keep you away from it. That is the fight you have to wage within yourselves, each one of you. The higher your development, the unhappier you must become if you do not follow the voice of your higher self, or, for that matter, the voices of divine spirits inspiring you.

These higher spirits can only be around you because your higher self has freed itself sufficiently, at least to some degree. If you do not heed these voices, if you let other considerations, whatever they may be, stand in your way, you must become unhappy. You will feel frustrated, you will have no peace of mind. If you choose to follow this voice, if you have decided to take this path and remain on it no matter what, happiness must be yours. But it is always the divine spark, the higher self that urges you on, and you will not find peace before you have found what you set out to find. He who knocks will enter; he who searches will find.

With that, my friends, I will return into my world. I leave you with God's blessings. May you be in peace. God is with you.

CHAPTER 15

Evil Equals Energy and Consciousness in Distortion

Greetings, all my friends here. Divine blessings and divine force pour forth from the world of spirit toward and into you, and from the deepest well within you to infuse your personality. However, this force must not be used to avoid what you do not want to see and know. It should be used to increase your honesty with yourself. For only then can love grow genuinely. And only then can you be secure within yourself and in the world.

In this lecture I will deal again with the concept of evil.

Some philosophies claim that there is no evil, that evil is an illusion. Others claim that evil is a fact observable by anyone who faces reality. Some religious philosophies contend that evil stems from one principal source, a specific entity called the devil —just as good stems from a personified God. Good and evil stem from two figures, according to this view. Still other philosophies say that the forces of good and evil exist as principles, as energy, as attitudes.

The various concepts of what evil is and where it comes from are all true, provided they do not exclude the apparently opposite approach. If you say that evil does not exist at all, on any level of being, this would be wrong. But if you state that in ultimate reality there is no evil, that is true. Any one of these postulates is incorrect when seen as the only truth. This may seem paradoxical, as is so often the case. But when we consider the question from a more profound and broader vantage point, what appear as opposites suddenly reconcile and complement each other.

The Universe Is Consciousness and Energy

I shall explain presently how these apparent opposites are all true. Let me first repeat that the universe consists of consciousness and energy. In the unified state, consciousness and energy are one. In the disunified state, they are not necessarily one. Energy can be an impersonal force that does not seem to contain or express consciousness. It seems a mechanical force that consciousness can direct but that is in itself alien to determination, to self-knowledge —in short, to everything that distinguishes consciousness. Think, for example, of electricity and atomic energy. Even the energy of mind often seems quite disconnected from the source of its consciousness. Perhaps you can feel what I mean, to a certain extent. For instance, many of you have experienced that the power of your thoughts, attitudes and feelings do not have an immediate effect in your life. They have indirect effect, which at first seems so disconnected from its source that comprehending the link between cause and effect requires focused attention and awareness. Only when your consciousness expands can you sense the oneness of this tremendous mind power and the energy it sets in motion. This oneness works in both a constructive and a destructive way. The principle is the same.

The separated, dualistic human mind creates the illusion that energy and consciousness are two different manifestations. The same split perception exists in human beings regarding life and self, God and humanity, cause and effect, and many other concepts or phenomena. There are people on this earth plane who experience the universe, the cosmos, as a purely energetic phenomenon. There are others who experience the universe, the cosmos, primarily as supreme consciousness. They are both right, of course. And they are both wrong when they claim that their view is the only truth. Both are one. Since thought is movement and energy, it is impossible to separate consciousness from energy in their essence, although in their manifestations there might be an apparent disconnection.

How can all the different philosophies and perceptions of life be true when they appear to be opposites? Let us look into this more closely. It is quite true that in the ultimate reality of the unified state there is no evil. Thought is pure and truthful; feelings are loving and blissful; the direction or intentionality of the will is utterly positive and constructive. Therefore there is no evil. But the same consciousness can change its mind, as it were, into an untruthful and limited thought process, accompanied by feelings of hate, fear, and cruelty, into negative will direction and intent. In that moment the same consciousness, or an aspect of this consciousness, turns into its own distorted version. If this happens, the energy also alters its manifestations.

Thus the manifestation of evil is not something intrinsically different from pure consciousness and energy. It has only changed direction or focus. Hence it is as accurate to state that in essence there is no evil as it is to state that on the level of the human manifestation there is.

Each individual must accept the reality of evil on this plane of development, in order to learn to cope with it and thus to truly overcome it. Evil must be faced and overcome primarily within the self. Only then can the evil that is outside of the self be dealt with. The attempt to reverse this process will fail, for everything must start from the inner center —and the center is the self.

In the present development of human consciousness, both the pure and the distorted, good and evil, God and the devil, exist. It is the task of every human being, on the long road of evolution, lifetime upon lifetime, to purify the soul and to overcome evil.

Evil Viewed as Consciousness and Energy

Let us look for a moment at what evil means, from the point of view both of energy and of consciousness. When energy is twisted, it produces a destructive manifestation. Its frequency slows down and becomes commensurate with the distortion of the consciousness which determines the state by choosing the will direction of the thought process and instituting the negative attitude pattern. The slower the movement, the more the distortion of consciousness has advanced, and the more we can speak of a manifestation of evil.

Another characteristic of distorted energy flow in its evil aberration is condensation. Condensed energy is the dualistic, disunified state. The more highly developed a being is, the purer is its energy, the faster its frequency and the more radiant its matter. The more distorted and destructive a being is, the more condensed is the form in which the consciousness manifests. Matter, as you know it, is an advanced state of condensation. The consciousness involved in this state must find its way back to an increased frequency of its energy movement by purifying its thought and attitude patterns.

What does evil mean as a phenomenon of consciousness?

Religion has of course talked amply about this with terms like hate, fear, selfishness, duplicity, spite, cheating life by not paying the price, wanting more than one is willing to give, and other destructive attitudes. This is obvious. But let us look at the phenomenon of evil on a more subtle level.

Jesus Christ said, "Do not resist evil." This saying has been misunderstood in many ways. It has been interpreted too literally to mean that you should allow others to exploit you and that you should not assert your human rights and your human dignity. Those who accept this interpretation have preached meekness and masochism that are not in keeping with divine truth. On the contrary, they help to perpetuate evil and allow the perpetrator to inflict evil on his or her environment.

Any truth can be interpreted in different correct ways. Since tonight we are discussing evil as a manifestation of consciousness and energy, I shall interpret "Do not resist evil" from this angle. "Do not resist evil" points to the fact that resistance itself is, and breeds, evil.

Unobstructed energy flows smoothly and harmoniously, like a gentle river. When there is resistance to the movement of the energy current, its movement slows and its form condenses, clogging up the channels. Resistance tightens and thus coarsens the energy. It holds back what should move.

Energy Thickens to Matter

The consciousness responsible for the energy thickening must exist accordingly. This statement is not quite correct, but human language is incapable of expressing the essential oneness of consciousness and energy, so we must compromise and speak as though consciousness were "responsible" for the energy flow. Anyhow, from your vantage point this expression will be quite adequate. The distorted thoughts, intentionality, feelings, and attitudes resist what is: truth, life, God —any aspect of the goodness of the universe. Because it resists trusting the life process, this consciousness generates ill will or negative intentionality. No evil attitude can manifest unless resistance to good is also taking place. Conversely, wherever life flows without resistance, it must be harmonious, blissful, and creative.

The very manifestation of matter as you know it, which is a highly disunified state, is the result of resistance. Matter is thickened, coarsened, slowed-down energy. Existence in matter blinds true vision and is therefore unavoidably painful. Resistance, matter, blindness, spells dualism, separation, evil, and suffering—these are one and the same. Resistance stems the flow, closing up; it prevents the movement of the universal energy —of love, of truth, of the ever-ongoing movement of life unfolding as divine manifestation.   Resistance is always obstructing some valuable, beautiful aspect of creation. Resistance is therefore a manifestation of evil.

When you go deeply enough into yourself, you will perceive your own resistance relatively easily. Others always can see it in you unless they are extremely blind or undeveloped, or insist on not seeing it. They may have a stake in agreeing with you or keeping an idealized image of you. But if this is not the case, they are aware of your resistance. You, too, can be aware of it if you wish to be. You will then see what this resistance means.

When you face and accept your deeply-ingrained negative intentionality, you can link it with your resistance. Resistance always says in one way or another, "I do not want to know the truth about this." This destructive attitude must create an evil force because it obstructs the ongoing movement of truth.

Self Will, Pride, and Fear

In our approach to self-development, we find again and again that the basic evil triad is pride, selfwill, and fear, which are always interconnected. All other manifestations of evil arise from this triad. Furthermore, each of these three attitudes is a result of resistance and breeds more resistance, or evil.

Selfwill says, "I resist any other way but my way," and "my way" is so often anti-life, anti-God. Selfwill resists truth, love, union —even if it appears to want it. The moment the tightness of selfwill exists, divine aspects are hindered from manifestation.

Pride is resistance to the oneness between entities. It separates itself from others and elevates itself —and thus resists the truth and love that are creative manifestations of life. Pride is the opposite of humility, not of humiliation. The person who resists humility must be humiliated because the resistance must always finally come to a breaking point. The refusal to expose the truth and to admit what exists is due to pride. This pride causes resistance as much as it results from resistance.

Similarly, resistance breeds fear, and fear breeds resistance. The tightened state of resistance and the slowing of the energy movement darken the vision and the scope of experience. Life is perceived as frightening. The more resistance, the more fear —and vice versa. Resistance to truth arises from the fear that truth can be harmful, and in turn, resistance to truth compounds this fear. The hiding becomes forever more difficult and exposure forever more threatening.

Fear of truth —hence resistance— negates the benign quality of the universe; it negates the truth of the self, with all its thoughts, feelings, and intents. This self-negation, rooted in resistance, is, and creates, evil.

When you want to avoid your feelings and your hidden thoughts and intentions, you create resistance. Resistance is, in one way or another, always connected with the thought, "I do not want to be hurt"—whether this hurt is actual or imagined. The resistance may be linked to selfwill that says, "I must not be hurt"; to pride that says, "I will never admit that I can be hurt"; or to fear that says, "If I am hurt I must perish." The resistance expresses distrust of the universe. In reality, hurt must pass, for it is no more an ultimate state than evil is. The more pain is experienced in its full intensity, the faster it dissolves into its original state— flowing, moving energy, which creates joy and bliss.

Whether resistance comes from selfwill, pride, or fear, whether it is ignorance or negation of what is, does not matter. Resistance obstructs God, the flow of life. It creates walls that separate you from truth and love —from your inner unity.

A person on the evolutionary path, who searches and gropes incarnation after incarnation —fulfilling his or her task, is in a conflicted inner state, as you know. A great deal in a human being like you is already free and developed. But there also exist in you distortion, blindness, ill will, resistance, evil.

Conflict and Crisis

The human being who is in a state of partial inner freedom—truth, love, and light on the one hand, and selfwill, pride, and fear on the other —must find the way out of this conflict. One part of the personality resists the truth that these negative feelings and attitudes are there and resists giving them up, while the other part strives for development and self-purification. This dualistic state must cause crisis. Let me repeat that such a crisis is unavoidable. When two opposite movements and strivings exist in a person, a breaking point must be reached, which manifests as a crisis in the person's life. One movement says, "Yes, I want to admit what is evil; I want to confront myself and dispense with the pretenses, which are after all nothing but lies.

I want to expand myself and bring forth the best in me, so that I can contribute and give to life, as I wish to receive from it. I want to give up the childish, cheating position from which I grab at life angrily and resentfully while refusing to give anything to it except my demands and resentments. I want to stop all that and ride trustfully with life. I want to honor God by accepting life on its own terms."

The other side persists in saying, "No. I want it my way. I may even want to develop and become decent and honest, but not at the price of looking at, exposing or admitting anything that is too self-incriminatory." The resulting crisis must break down the faulty inner structure.

Where the destructive orientation is considerably weaker than the constructive one, the crisis is relatively minor, for the faulty aspects can be extricated without tearing down the entire psychic edifice. By the same token, if the movement toward growth and truth is considerably weaker than the stagnant, resistive, evil one, major crisis may again be avoided for a while; the personality may stagnate for long periods. But when the movement toward good is sufficiently strong, and yet the resistance continues to block the movement of the whole personality —which becomes confused, blind and caught in destructive acting-out — something must give.

Constructive Destruction

Suppose you build a house. Some of the building material is solid, beautiful, and of excellent quality. Some is defective, a cheap imitation, and rotten. When these two incompatible types of material become inextricably mixed, the structure cannot stand. If the rotten material can be extricated without tearing down the entire building, then profound shake-up of the inhabitants' present life can be avoided. So it is with a personality —and such extrication depends entirely on the conscious determination of the person in question. If the personality is too entangled because it has been resisting for too long and still lacks sufficient impetus of goodwill, there is only one way out. The structure must be destroyed so that it can be rebuilt in a pure form.

Such a process calls forth an energy movement that is almost impossible to describe. Resisting evil means not facing and accepting the evil in you. This resistance creates a tremendous accumulation of energy, which finally comes to an explosion.

The deeper meaning of the ensuing destruction is truly marvelous. It destroys the very evil that has created it. Unfortunately it is impossible to convey the configuration that takes place. Much in the person's life may go to pieces. The energy movement of the soul substance tears down the rotten structure, even if this means that temporarily all seems to go to pieces. However, what is of true value will automatically and organically rebuild itself.

Imagine a form composed of intense opposite movements that swirl and rush, explode and implode and destroy themselves. Soul substance is torn apart and rebuilds itself simultaneously. Creation is taking place. Every crisis is an integral part of creation. Therefore, wise ones embrace and accept crises, which remove more and more resistance. Do not resist evil in you. By that I mean, give up the appearance, the pretense that evil does not exist in you. Give in, go with the movement of life.

The process of destruction/creation is a magnificent sight for spirit eyes. The blind entity may suffer temporarily, but how good it is. The process is awesome in its benign violence. New movements come forth; old movements change direction, color, hue, sound.

If you go deeply into yourself and intuitively feel into the meaning of your crisis, you may gain a glimmer of the creative process. It is simultaneously both creative and destructive, as far as defective soul material is concerned.

The eternal, ultimate, essentially benign nature of creation is most eloquently demonstrated in the fact that evil must finally destroy itself. It can build up only for so long, but eventually the breakdown must occur. You will all agree that the destruction of destructiveness is a constructive, creative phenomenon.

Thus, in the long run, every destruction is constructive and serves creation. Always. But in an individual's life, this truth is not always obvious. The further you are on the path, the more you will see this truth. It will be helpful if you can meditate to truly experience this phenomenon, because then you will aid the process by your conscious determination to relinquish resisting the evil in you, which you mistakenly believe comes to you from outside.

You can diminish the violence of the constructive destruction if your commitment to truth takes on a new impetus and if you unearth your *negative intentionality* and change it into a *positive intentionality* [8]. When you express negative intentionality in concise words, you can create a new movement. It is up to you. But even before you do so, by your very admission of your deliberate ill will, you will be more in truth and less inclined to act out the evil, which you sometimes even do self-righteously. You will know who you are. And strangely enough, the more you own up to your evil, the more honorable you become, and the more you will know that and appreciate yourself.

It is the same with pain: The more you accept it, the less you will feel it. Resistance to pain often makes it unbearable. The more you accept your hate, the less you hate. The more you accept your ugliness, the more beautiful you become. The more you accept your weakness, the stronger you are. The more you admit your hurt, the more dignity you have, regardless of the distorted views of others. These are inexorable laws. This is the path we tread.

Now, my friends, continue in your wonderful endeavor to be in truth. If your sincerity is doubted, you must know in your heart where you are —and that is all that matters. That is all that matters! Be blessed. Be who you truly are!

---

8. See Glossary for definition of **positive and negative intentionality**.

CHAPTER 16

Three Principles
of Evil

My dearest friends, God's blessings envelop you.

In this lecture I wish to instruct you again about certain realities and laws concerning evil. It is very important that you understand more about this controversial subject at this present moment. For many centuries the power of evil was fully recognized. Humanity had a sense of the invisible, and of what is usually referred to as the supernatural regarding both the forces of light and the forces of darkness, as well as their manifestations, their effects, their influence in your realm, and their personification as spirit entities —as angels and as devils.

It has always been said that the individual's free will determined whose influence would predominate in one's life. While human beings were still in their immature mental and emotional states, their wills were not sufficiently developed to make conscious, appropriate, and wise choices. The strength of their lower selves and their inability and unwillingness to face and therefore transcend the lower self, frequently made them prey to evil influences. Lack of self-knowledge inevitably led to lack of self-responsibility. Thus humanity felt victimized by evil spirits. Fear of them often led to submission to them —and this happened on a quite conscious and intentional level. The worship of Satan occurred openly. And when this was not the case, it certainly occurred unconsciously by choosing the influences that corresponded to the intentionality of the lower self.

As history proceeded, a disconnection from the invisible world occurred. This disconnection itself is a manifestation of evil which I shall explain more specifically later. Now I just want to say what I have often mentioned before: Evil and its manifestation must itself become the medicine to overcome evil —at least in the long run. Therefore this disconnection from supernatural realities inevitably had very regrettable effects. But it also created an arena in which people could no longer blame the devil for their own misdemeanors. They had to look within themselves to correct the effects of evil. So humanity had to go through a period of isolation and separateness from the invisible realities in order to grow into self-responsibility. However, what was ridiculed as superstition was in reality a half-truth. It is indeed a kind of superstition when outside forces are made responsible for one's fate. The other side of this picture is the fact that these invisible forces do exist and do have their influences.

In other words, we are dealing once again with a duality: Either the self is responsible for the individual's fate or the angels and devils are. Humanity has matured sufficiently to be able to unite this duality. After a long period of concentrating on the self at the expense of invisible forces, the time has come when you can combine the two facets of reality and truly make them the one reality that it is from our spirit-world's vantage point.

Although I have discussed the existence of these forces ever since my task with you began, for a considerable time we concentrated mostly on your own inner being with all its subtleties and all the various levels of consciousness and their interaction within you and around you. Occasionally I did of course return to the power of these forces, but always in conjunction with your own determining voice. You have begun to understand that to the degree your lower self is conscious, thereby enabling you to choose not to act upon it and to pray for help to purify it, to that degree you are *invulnerable to evil*. To the degree you commit yourself to the will of the highest and dedicate your life to follow in Christ's footsteps, to that degree evil spirits cannot approach you. But it is not enough to voice such good intentions on the surface of your being. This decision must penetrate the most hidden levels of your personality if you are to become the shining light that repels dark spirits. The purification process of this path is a deep-rooted system that totally renews the personality on all levels.

My beloved friends, the time has come for you to understand more profoundly how you are an electromagnetic field that always attracts what is commensurate with certain levels of your innermost being. In order to attain this awareness completely and clearly, you need more information. For this reason I should now like to discuss three specific principles of evil. Your understanding of this material will prove immensely useful and will bring into clearer focus your view of life in general and of your own life in particular.

Separation

The first of the three basic principles of evil is the most obvious to humanity. The devil was always associated with this principle, which aims to destroy and to inflict suffering at all cost. The *separation* between the self that perpetrates suffering and the victim who suffers is so great that the perpetrator is deluded into being unaffected by the further effects of his or her acts. It is known that everything about Satan is earmarked by separation —not only from God, but also from others and from the self. This aspect of separation exists in the case of all three principles I shall discuss here. The delusion of evil in the case of this first principle lies in the denial that your brother's or sister's pain is unavoidably also your own pain. Instead of recognizing this basic truth, a person filled with evil, whether in human form or as a discarnate entity, experiences excitement and pleasure when spreading destruction, suffering, and pain.

Materialism

The second principle of evil is *materialism*. This applies not only to the earth sphere, but equally and often even more to a variety of hellish spheres in which entities live in a totally disconnected way, convinced that the dead state of thickly condensed matter —much more thickly condensed than your living matter—is the only reality that exists. In such hellish spheres the suffering is not the same as the suffering deriving from the first principle, which was often depicted by visionaries in your earthly sphere. This second principle is less often understood and sensed. Visionaries have not seen the spheres corresponding to and manifesting this principle.

I'll give one illustration. Imagine a life in which nature is totally absent. Nothing is alive; all is condensed matter. Nothing has flavor. By the same token the entity's inner nature is equally inaccessible. Everywhere there is only deadness, mechanicalness, and alienation from all that is pulsating life, within and without. There is no birth and no death, yet the unchanging existence here is not the eternal life that is truly heavenly. This manifestation is the distortion of eternity. It is hopelessness itself as if no change were ever possible. Existence is totally mechanical. Such a hopeless kind of suffering is neither more nor less desirable than suffering through direct infliction of pain. It is simply a suffering of a different kind corresponding to a different principle of evil.

It should be easy to see that until fairly recently in your history your earth sphere manifested the first principle of evil in a much stronger way. In the last hundred years or so, the influence of the second principle has become stronger. With the disappearance of superstition, the connection with the subliminal levels of reality also disappeared. The life line to pulsating reality and reenlivening was broken. The result was an alienated reality in which humanity prided itself on its advanced state— advanced because the emphasis on matter actually did result in technological progress, but also "advanced" because human beings became the only reality unto themselves. This had its positive and negative ramifications. The positive manifestation brought people back to taking responsibility for themselves, and therefore led them to search within themselves, to an ever increasing degree, for the causes of their fate. It is not coincidental that at this point the human psyche became a matter of scientific study, with psychology as a helpful tool in this endeavor. The negative manifestation was that a life was produced which is not totally different from the first sphere of evil I described.

These two principles have been known by spiritually aware people. Since every principle and every aspect of spiritual reality can and frequently does also manifest as an entity, two different kinds of devils were also recognized by some visionaries. They represented and personified these two principles. Each one held its own kingdom and ruled its own world with many spirits of lesser power serving it. The hierarchy that is recognized in divine spheres also exists in satanic spheres.

Confusion and Half-Truth

The third principle of evil is little known. Although it has been recognized only in a vague way, perhaps as a by-product of evil but hardly ever as a powerful principle itself, it is as effective as the other two principles. Like them it also has its own personification, hierarchy, and realm. It is the principle of *confusion*, distortion, *half-truth*, and all the variations that may possibly exist in connection with it. It includes using truth where it does not belong or is not applicable, so that the truth subtly turns into a lie without being easily traced as such because it is presented under the guise of divine truth and seems unassailable. The resulting confusion is not just an extremely effective weapon of evil; it is an evil principle in itself.

It will be easy to see, my friends, how important it is for you to understand this now. You will find all these principles represented in your world, around you and within your own lower self. You will see that in its negative intentionality your own lower self contains all three principles of evil. Only when you become clearly aware of this can you recognize when devilish forces and spirits want to destroy you and inflict pain on you by enticing you to inflict pain on others. They also want to convince you of the illusion that you are separated and isolated, that neither God nor any life exists beyond the life of your present body. Finally, they want to drive you crazy with confusion, dualistic splits, false either/ors, half-truths, and subtle distortions that you cannot sort out. To recognize all this is of tremendous value for you. You cannot deal with an enemy whose existence you ignore and whose weapons you cannot recognize.

The time has come when you can clearly see how the corresponding type of distortion in the unpurified areas of your soul becomes an inevitably compelling field of attraction to powerful forces of evil. You can neutralize these forces and render them harmless only by your own determination to remain true to God. You can use the light of Christ to help you work within yourself and purify yourself so that this field of attraction within you can be transformed into a different magnet attracting different forces.

It must also be understood that these principles always coexist but one may be stronger in manifestation at certain periods of history or during certain phases of an individual's life. It is the individual characteristics and personal inclinations of each entity that determine which of these three principles are most compatible with the individual in question. Collectively speaking, at different periods in the cycle of evolution, one or the other of these principles will be most prevalent. That does not mean that the other two principles will be absent. They all contribute to the ultimate aim of the forces of darkness: To alienate creation from the Creator.

Here is an example of how this interaction of the three principles works. Confusion and distortion of reality —making a truth out of a lie and a lie out of the truth —create a numbness toward the cosmic, eternal aliveness that can be felt deep in the soul of any individual when there is truth and clarity. This numbness, created out of confusion and chaos, inevitably inflicts pain and suffering just as the lie must inflict pain and suffering. Starting with any one of the three principles most prevalent in an individual or in a collective manifestation, you will see that they must all coexist and reinforce one another.

Good and Evil Personified

Today's human mentality can accept the principle of good and evil more easily than the fact that they are both also personified. However, even the principle of good and evil is still often disputed, as if good or evil were merely subjective perceptions. Here again we are dealing with a half-truth. In fact, both good and evil are often experienced on a very superficial level according to limited, personal, and highly subjective perceptions. When the issues are seen on a deeper level of consciousness, what was first believed to be good can often be seen as questionable and possibly as a mask of something evil. By the same token, what appears bad on the surface might turn out to be a very good experience or manifestation. So it is quite true that good and evil should be both viewed with caution and discernment and examined in as much depth as possible.

However, it is a grave mistake to assume that because of this fact good and evil do not exist in a very real way. The denial of good and evil as absolutes, in spite of the relative perception humans have of them, leads to nihilism, hopelessness, and the void —as if that were the ultimate reality. For quite a while it was considered very fashionable and intelligent to postulate this nihilism. It obviously expresses the same separation from deeper and cosmic realities as the second principle of materialism. The confusion and half-truth inherent in the denial of absolute good and evil is an expression of the third principle which breeds the second principle, until that ultimately causes the first principle.

In this age, humanity has made a step in the right direction because it begins to recognize that good and evil actually exist above and beyond the relativity that is due to limited human perception. Humanity is open to accepting God as a creative principle and also sees the existence of another principle that countermands the divine creative principle. But people nowadays are still very hesitant to accept that all principles can and do manifest as entities. It is as though you still hesitated to let yourself be called childish and primitive by people who believe themselves to be wiser and more knowledgeable when they ridicule other manifestations of reality.

If personification of principles and creative forces did not exist, how could you exist as human beings? A human being is merely one form of personification. You personify both principles of good and evil, as you now know very well. Why should it be so hard to accept, or why should it appear so primitive and unintelligent to believe that along the scale of development there exist beings who manifest more or less of each principle? And finally, why should there not exist entities who manifest total goodness and total badness? In the latter instance you may say that all created beings are ultimately divine, so they cannot be all bad. This is true in a much wider sense, but it is possible that in their present state of manifestation their divine core is so overlaid by evil that nothing of it manifests. We are here to deal with the fact that personification does exist in all gradations, and to deny this would be far from knowledgeable or intelligent. Knowing that angels surround and influence you need not lead to worshipping the angels and overlooking Jesus Christ — the divine manifestation as personification —who is the ultimate source of all you need and of your life itself. You need not overlook that direct contact with Jesus Christ is what opens the channel of communication between Him and you. Nor should such awareness of spiritual presence lead you to fear the devils you sporadically attract according to certain cyclic rhythms.

Devils Are Cause, Effect and Medicine

Like all disease, the devils near you are cause, effect, and medicine. Their proximity and their effect on you is caused by your own unpurified, limited, and undeveloped consciousness. Your unpurified consciousness has the effect of drawing devils near you whose lies confuse you so that you no longer know what is truth and what is untruth. Your confusion induced by them can be used by you as a medicine, if you so choose. You can use it as an indication that you need to develop and purify these unattended parts of your soul. Instead of fearing the devils or denying their existence so you can overcome your fear, you need to recognize their voices and learn to distinguish where these voices come from. This is in itself a very necessary step in your development. If you ignore or deny their existence, how in the world can you become aware of them and counteract them? If you do not know that at times they surround you and inspire you, you unknowingly become their tool. If you do not consider that lies may be whispered into your thinking apparatus, you will not use your capacity to question and doubt the thoughts that filter through you.

It is necessary to become aware of the connection between your lower self— which, due to its ignorance, fear, and lack of faith, creates destructive defenses and negative intentionality— and the voices of satanic entities. Together these two sources of negativity wreak havoc in your life and in the lives of those around you. The time has come when you need to know clearly, fearlessly, and intelligently what the facts of life are in this respect. Because the stronger you become in your higher self and its positive intentionality, while at the same time leaving certain aspects of the lower self unattended to, the more you become prey to evil influences who are much more interested in you than with those who are not particularly aware of subliminal forces and whose life is not dedicated to God.

Now is the time when you particularly need to know as much as possible of the enemy and its weapons, so that you can combat this enemy force which is drawn toward you whenever you do not heed these periods of contact and fail to decide to make them a medicine.

The Laws Governing Evil

It is often not understood that Satan does not regard God, the source of all life, the creative principle of all universes, as the opponent against whom all his efforts and warfare are directed. Satan, the ultimate personification of all evil containing all three principles personified as entities, recognizes God as creator and bends to His will and His laws. He cannot help doing so. It was God's will for evil to have its sphere of activity and influence, for only in this way can evil be truly overcome within the soul of all fallen spirits, all entities who have chosen thoughts and actions that plunged them into darkness. It is to ensure this ultimate overcoming of evil that very exacting laws and rules exist, preventing Satan from acting outside these laws. Definite limits are being set, always according to the will and choice of the individuals in question.

If God, the creative principle of all universes, is not the enemy of personified evil, who then is? It is God in the manifest personification of the Christ. His light of truth and of eternal life is unbearable to all satanic spirits. This same light will inspire you with truth and life, will connect you with the source of all life and will light up your path. But you must make the decision whether you wish this Christ light to shine on your way and make following the light of Christ your way, or whether you unwittingly wish to submerge yourself in thoughts of untruth and confusion because momentarily this seems easier, and perhaps even more pleasurable and exciting.

Satan's Opponent Is Christ

Satan's real opponent is Jesus Christ, who came to open a way for all creatures captivated and weakened by satanic influences. This has to do precisely with the fact of personification. When the Christ manifested God as man, thus being both divine and human, He accomplished the greatest feat imaginable. He proved that it was possible to remain true to God, true to truth, and not succumb to the strongest of influences and temptations that the personification of evil could unleash. Through this tremendous act of steadfastness, the man who was God manifest and the God who had put on human nature opened the doors in the souls of all created beings. He forged ahead, enabling those who were submerged in darkness to find their way gradually back to light. Jesus Christ has saved every single entity who ever was created and every particle of consciousness and energy that ever manifested and ever will manifest as personality. Since He came to earth the great light is always available for the building of a tunnel to the world of light.

When satanic entities encounter this Christ light, they suffer physical pain. All divine attributes are contained in this light, and the light of truth stings evil spirits. The light of love is unbearably oppressive to them, and the light of positive aggression is fearsome and terrifying. Only God manifest can become visible and perceivable to other personifications. God's other aspect, the unmanifest divine principle, can be only indirectly experienced by personalized energy/consciousness units.

The great light of the cosmic Christ reaches a soul in darkness at first through pain. To some degree all of you on this path have experienced this occasionally, to a much lesser degree of course than the dark spirits. You have come in touch with a reaction which at first seems inexplicable, where you recoil from happiness, fulfillment, pleasure, and love. You close up your centers of receptivity against God's abundance. First this puzzles you, but later you learn to see and observe this reaction in you, just as you learn to observe any other irrational and destructive reaction. Often this seems to make so little sense that you become discouraged when you see this reaction in you again and again. You meditate; you visualize yourself being receptive to happiness, love, and fulfillment; and yet this automatic reaction continues.

Is it not clear to you yet that the hidden part of your lower self that resists exposure and transformation is unable to allow the personality to stand the light? So prayer is not enough, neither is good will and meditation, visualization and logic. None of them will make you really accessible to the light as long as a hidden agenda exists in your soul. In that area you must react similarly to demonic entities who hide from the light of Christ, a light which contains all happiness, eternal fulfillment, and life itself. This hidden area makes you react with pain to this light. In this area you become connected to the forces of darkness and you are a target for them.

When you observe your own similar reactions of contraction, restlessness, and anxiety when great pleasure and fulfillment come to you, you can then connect with the principle I am trying to convey here. And you will understand very well what I mean when I discuss the demonic spirits' flight from Christ's light. You will also comprehend what history has tried to convey again and again: that Christ is the great adversary of Satan.

The Battle Waged in Every Soul

What exists in microcosm with the human soul also exists in the macrocosm. Every inner drama is a reflection of an outer drama and vice versa. Every battle within the human soul between the forces of light and of darkness, between the higher self and the lower self, is also waged on a universal level, enacted by many entities at different stages of development. Every personality goes through this battle within himself or herself; every personality experiences it occasionally in his or her surroundings; and, last but not least, every personality will become involved in larger issues that also represent this universal battle between good and evil.

The individual's role in this battle—on whatever level it

takes place —very much depends on his or her conscious, deliberate choice of where he or she wants to be. When issues are tinged by personal emotions, desires, or interests that belong to the realm of darkness, and these personal emotions are not recognized as fogging the vision, then one truly becomes a target for one or all of the three principles of evil. Cruelty will be hidden under the guise of expressing your feelings, while maligning and distortion will become the tools of cruelty and the intent to hurt. Disconnection from deeper reality will blind you to the true meaning of events. Confusion will be rampant so that truth will be used for lying and lies will be called the truth. The forces of evil have been allowed to find entrance through your lower self which you have not dealt with sufficiently.

My dearest friends, do not allow yourselves to become enmeshed in this battle: Do not unwittingly lend yourselves as tools for the aims of the Prince of Darkness. Use your good will to see the truth. See both the truth of your hidden lower-self motives and the truth of your higher-self good will. Give up the line of least resistance and its negative pleasure, which makes you persist in a destructive course bringing clouds of pain and darkness to you and those around you. The key is really quite simple. It is so tempting to follow negative thoughts and come to believe them. But this furthers a lower-self fixation to indulge in the negative pleasure of negative thoughts, suspicions, blames, and accusations which may or may not be true.

Clarification will come when the truth is really wanted, even if a part of the truth at this moment is still that you do not want the truth, that you want to attack, to blame, to see people or events in the worst light. The reason why you secretly wish for this can be explored only when you no longer deny feeling this way. The truth will shimmer through slowly but inexorably, once you admit a negative intentionality which then attracts expert spirits of lying and of confusion. Clarity will dissolve the pain of your guilt that is frequently not allowed to surface. You keep it down by strengthening the destructive process of projecting on others what you fear in yourself. Clarity will also help dissolve the pain you inflict on others with this evil projection.

Do not ever delude yourself into believing that negative intent and negative thoughts do not inevitably reflect in your actions and affect others in an insidious way. Thoughts can never remain separated things. They create results and events in one form or another. Clarity will come from honestly pursuing and answering the above questions after you have delved into your hidden thought processes, which are seldom completely unconscious. This clarity will dissolve the pain. It will re-establish your connection with eternal life.

You are all reaching the point in your development when taking responsibility for your creation must be combined with a profound knowledge of the invisible worlds and the laws according to which you attract or repel entities of different nature and development who then influence you and reinforce the force field within your soul. Each of the many areas of your soul may be influenced by the highest or by the lowest forces. The choice is up to you.

It is also important to understand that a person does not experience temporary evil influences because he or she is undeveloped, or evil, or bad. One individual may be more accosted by evil even though what needs to be purified in his or her soul may be much less dark than another person's soul substance who may be less accosted by demonic influences. I mean this in an absolute sense. The law of attraction and repulsion is purely relative here. For example, if you have reached a comparatively high level of development, the areas that remain to be transformed and are not recognized by your consciousness— even though they may not be particularly destructive or outright wrong—exert through their unrecognized parts a greater attraction to evil than does the negative charge of a person who is on an altogether lower plane of development. It would be good if you pondered this law and could feel into an understanding of it.

With this, my dearest ones, I give all of you the blessings of truth and love. The light I bring is always the light of Christ. He has said He is the truth and He is the way and He is life. In His light you find the way to truth in the smallest and largest issues, in personal and impersonal issues. This way leads to the love of the Creator who has given eternal life. Eternal life can be found only in truth. The way to the truth leads through the mazes of the dark areas in your own soul; through encountering the temptation to remain in them and savor their passing gratification; through the deliberate overcoming of this temptation. The great Christ light is the overpowering love of the Creator, of Creation, of all that is. Be blessed; choose this way.

Part Seven

Approaching the Unitive State

"What good is it to me for the Creator to give
birth to his Son if I do not also give birth
to him in my time and my culture?
This then, is the fullness of time:
When the Son of God is begotten in us."

—*Meister Eckhart*

We will now be given a preview of what our experiences may be as we get closer and closer to full realization of the unitive state. The following three lectures show us what to expect and what feelings and sensations we will begin to have, so that we can recognize what is happening to us and thereby not push away experiences which we otherwise might fear. For what is beginning to happen is really the culmination of all our labors.

In the later stages of the work we will have learned to reconcile our split-off ego with our real self. This is the crucial beginning step in transcending duality and truly experiencing the unitive principle. When we do so we recognize the truth that our own interests are *not ever* in opposition to the interests of others.

Prior to this awareness, over-identification with the ego made power a dangerous weapon, in opposition to love. After the ego and real self are united, this shifts: Power and love can now work together. From this position of not struggling and not forcing, one can then begin to *consciously re-create one's life*. This re-creation arises from harmonizing with one's real needs, rather than trying to meet false needs defined by the separate ego. When you are aligned with this task in faith and patience, "all restlessness disappears and a deep sense of meaning and ful-fillment comes into your soul."

The second lecture in this section gives an inspiring descrip-tion of the cosmic feeling that comes to us more and more as we begin to glimpse the unitive state: "It is an experience of bliss, of the comprehension of life and its mysteries, of all-encompassing love; of the knowledge that all is well and there is nothing to fear." This experience obviously far transcends our little, personal self; it both arises from and strengthens our real, integrated self. In this state it is possible for us to know fully what is real and what is illusion. The bulk of this lecture is devoted to presenting four keys to attaining this state— important guides for our work at this stage.

The lecture on Jesus Christ teaches us that in this latter stage of the work we will, if we are open to it, come into personal contact with Christ. This is not a statement that we *should* experience Christ, or that we are supposed to strain ourselves in some way to make this happen. Rather, we are assured that as we grow closer to surrendering to the will of God, personal contact with Christ *enables* us to be braver and go further in our work of honesty, self-exposure and transformation. If we pray to be open to Christ, a time will come when we will feel, strongly and personally, His presence, assistance, and love — when we can, through Him, "create a healthy center of gravity anchored deeply within our soul."

D.T.

CHAPTER 17

Your Capacity to Create

Greetings and blessings for every one of you here.

I will speak about the human capacity to create, an astoundingly underestimated potentiality. Your creative ability is infinitely greater than you and your scientists, psychologists or philosophers realize. With the exception of a very few enlightened ones, most people do not know of their dormant capacity to create and recreate their lives. Some may believe in it in theory, but few have truly experienced it.

When you adopt a human body and the ego state in this three-dimensional world, you automatically close off the memory of other states of consciousness. These forgotten states are much less confined, much freer, much more aware. In them you were completely capable of molding your life, to a degree that the human consciousness cannot possibly comprehend.

A Map into Your Inner Regions

The power of thoughts, feelings and attitudes is enormous. This power exists just as much now, in your present state, but you do not see it. You do not know that you have molded what you experience in this moment in such a precise way that there can be no mistake concerning it. As I have often said, the sum total of all your conscious, semi-conscious, unconscious, explicit and implicit thoughts, beliefs, assumptions, intentions, feelings, emotions and will directions —conflicting as they may be creates your present experience and the way your life unfolds for you. Your present life expresses your inner state exactly, like a faultless mathematical equation. Thus you can use your life as a map into your inner regions. This is, after all, part of the method of the pathwork.

Many of you have verified that hidden, feared, guilt-producing and denied thoughts and feelings are more powerful in their negative creation than anything you deal with on the conscious level. Fear and guilt are potent creative agents. They contain a great deal of energy. On the positive level, enthusiasm, joy, vitality, interestedness, stimulation are also potent energy agents.

A path such as this must therefore be intensely concerned with exploring what you believe, feel, assume and intend on layers of your personality that are not immediately accessible. Your unconscious motives often create what you do not wish to experience at all because you do not know what you bargain for and what side-effects are attached to your unwise wishes, false assumptions and negative intents. Also, you ignore the potency of such psychic material and do not see how infallibly it translates itself into the creation of matter, of events and circumstances, and of life experiences.

When you adopt the limited human ego state, you do so for very specific purposes. You manifest and express yourself in this limited state for the purpose of purification and unification. It would not be possible to do such work as quickly and as effectively if you were in full possession of your entire consciousness and your faculties, my friends. For your ego personality, as it expresses itself now, is but an isolated aspect, or several isolated aspects, of your total personality. A much larger, fuller and more purified part of your total personality, or real self, does not manifest overtly. The manifestation of certain aspects in an isolated form—which consists of the three-dimensional reality and the ego—affords possibilities of a focused awareness that is lacking when these unpurified aspects are submerged in the largely purified personality. Your purified spirit can easily overlook small but significant distortions that nevertheless act as hindrances to further developments surpassing the scope of human consciousness. Such developments proceed in spheres of reality that you cannot comprehend now.

It is, however, possible to activate the capacities of the larger self, to focus on it and be receptive to its ever-present inner voice. Similarly, it is possible to focus on and be receptive to negative aspects of your personality that lie deeply buried and that need to be purified on your evolutionary road. This path teaches you to contact all these hidden layers and deal with them appropriately. In other words, some parts of you are more developed and others less. The latter are not manifest, but they are still you. The manifest, more developed part has the means to explore, bring out and unify the other parts which you cannot yet see.

When you undertake this exploration as your main task in life, all restlessness disappears and a deep sense of meaning and fulfillment comes into your soul. Slowly but surely life's frustrations begin to disappear and rich fulfillment begins to take their place. For only when you focus your attention on the reason for coming into this plane in the first place can you find your place in life.

Divine Laws in Distortion

Whatever divine laws and attributes exist in the universe, the moment they express themselves in the isolated ego state, disconnected from deeper inner reality, they become distorted and destructive. Let me give you an example.

A small child believes that it is omnipotent. Psychology designates this very obvious expression of the infant's claim to omnipotence as immaturity and destructive egocentricity. It is that, but it is also much more. The feeling of omnipotence is a memory of another state, a state of consciousness in which, indeed, thoughts become things and events the moment they are formed. Time and distance are part of the three-dimensional, illusory state of consciousness, so they do not exist in a realm of much more expanded consciousness. The consciousness of the infant is still partially tuned in on the state of its total being. However, as the memory is translated into the confined and limited ego state, it comes out jumbled.

Since the ego state is a concentration of the less purified state— in combination with already purified aspects which come to the aid of the personality in the task of this life— the power to create takes on a distorted, undesirable form. The ego always lives in the illusion that it is not only separate from others, but that others are essentially antagonistic to its well-being. Everything the ego does is always either against or in competition or in comparison with others. This is what creates its destructiveness and egocentricity. The ego makes power a dangerous weapon, as you all well know. You experience power as something you fear in others and feel guilty about in yourself. Power is thus always exclusive of love and joy, for it is an intensely separating expression.

But when you conciliate your ego-split with the real self and thus discover the unitive principle, you discover that your interest is never in opposition to the interests of others, although on a superficial level it may first appear that way. You also discover that power and love need not be opposites. You can then begin to use your innate power to create and recreate your life. You may now understand better why knowledge of your power to create is dangerous as long as you have not purified the distorted aspect that has found expression in this body and in this life, and as long as you have not discovered the eternal inner realities, which are much more real than what you consider outer reality.

The infant's frustration when its thoughts and wishes do not instantly become fact is obvious. The immediacy of cause and effect —cause being the thought or wish, effect being the experience —is a constant "given" in the state of consciousness that goes beyond the ego. One of the tasks of most humans as isolated ego aspects is to learn trustful patience, flowing with the stream, unwillful receptivity.

Memory of the power to create must be temporarily cut off so that you can learn what you came here to learn. Through the very learning of this lesson the deeper connections establish themselves again spontaneously. However, it does not seem to be rediscovered memory. Instead, connecting thoughts, wishes, intents, feelings and attitudes with experience seems to be a new discovery that establishes awareness of the power to create. Then there is no longer the danger of using power against others. The illusion that self-interest must be against the interest of others is pierced.

I hardly need to mention that not only actual infants make egocentric and antagonistic claims to omnipotence. Undeveloped, immature and destructive people do too, and they often act them out.

Converting Negative to Positive

Wherever there are misconceptions, ignorance, false ideas, and withheld emotional matter —spite, stubbornness, rigidity, inertia—stagnant energy exists that must create disturbance and negative experiences. It is very potent energy. Only when you release it directly and honestly can you transform this energy.

The time has come when you can convert negative energy and consciousness into positive manifestation. To some extent you have actually begun to do so, but you are not yet sufficiently aware of the power of the energy as it is released. If, at the moment the negative energy is leaving your system and begins to flow, you can reconvert it and direct it into a positive channel, you can indeed bring new creation into your life. This practice will make you understand how much creative power you have.

These words will not be enough to convey the truth to you in a real way unless you have overcome certain attitudes of separateness. Otherwise, this knowledge would be dangerous for you and for others. But totally committing to the path into your own inner regions with all its apparent hardship of self-revelation and self-confrontation will make you increasingly aware of the spiritual reality of your own state of eternal being that cannot die. You will also become aware of the power of your thoughts, your intent, your feelings. You will learn to be careful what thoughts you think without either repressing or suppressing undesirable and destructive thoughts. You will learn to deal with such material, to challenge its accuracy and be open to other alternatives. Learn to understand what it is in you that makes you want to think that way and what price you pay. Begin to see creation as the relationship between the causes and effects that you have always seen as unrelated.

As this growing process proceeds, re-creation takes place. It is not a reward for good behavior. It is a simple act, instituted by the self that is now in a much increased state of awareness, that now knows what it is doing and why.

Focusing constructively on the undeveloped aspects in you means that you fulfill the task for which you came into this particular world. It means that you unify yourself so that you can actualize your potent creative power and use it consciously and deliberately in your life now.

The creative process and the specific techniques to learn are given to you slowly. I have shown you some techniques of meditation. When you meditate, you create. In this concentrated, relaxed state, energy and consciousness focus in such a way that powerful creative seeds are released. When a certain foundation of inner self-purification and self-awareness exists, these techniques can be expanded. It will then be safe, from the point of view of this spiritual path. Your being will then truly be grounded in reality and in a unifying process, so that you will not ignore any aspect you have come to fulfill.

The organic process of learning creative meditation, re-creating life experience, will come as an intuitive, spontaneous expansion of your consciousness. Just as you will intuitively understand cosmic reality from experience rather than theory, so will you learn to avail yourself of your innate powers and resources.

I would like to elucidate an inner mechanism that is extremely important for you to understand. My friends, working on this path you must have experienced quite frequently that your *helper*[9] may suggest a specific meditation and commitment in meditation to a positive self-expression that you deeply desire because you miss it. Yet as you pursue that self-expression, you experience an inexplicable resistance to follow through. Something in you seems to stop you, or you forget to do it on your own. It simply does not occur to you. Perhaps your thoughts have no energy, conviction or clarity. They are diffuse and you feel that they have little effect. At times you may even consciously experience an outright resistance to meditate for the very thing you most desire. What is this block?

Let us suppose you are lonely. Let us suppose you long for a full and fruitful partnership—an abundance of joy, of exchange, of sharing, of mutuality on every level. You do have the birthright to experience this and other fulfillments, for the universe's abundance is there for everyone. No one is excluded. Nevertheless, it may hardly even occur to you to actively sow the seed in meditation —by a clear, definite thought in that direction, and by a commitment to wanting it, to experiencing it, to realizing and bringing this experience into actuality. You may be perfectly aware of the principle of such meditative practice; nevertheless you desist from employing it. What is even more significant is that when, upon suggestion, you do formulate the creative thought pattern, you find a strange and inexplicable reluctance in yourself. It is as though a wall in you prevented you from the clear, concise commitment to what you most ardently yearn for.

Have you ever thought about the meaning of this resistance? You want something desperately. You intrinsically believe it could exist for you. Your mind accepts the principles of creation. Yet you will find your mind strangely paralyzed when it comes to truly letting go of your thoughts, to sending your thoughts into the fertile soil of the creative substance, or what I call the soul substance, where any seed will grow to fruition.

The reason for this reluctance is very simple. It is the self-protective, finely calibrated mechanism that knows that some-

---

9. A **helper** is a committed Pathworker trained to help others in their work of self-purification.

thing in you is not yet ready for this experience. You yourself have put obstructions in the way. Perhaps there is an unwillingness to give and to accept reality on your level. Perhaps there is a concealed negative attitude toward the other sex you are not prepared to resolve. Whatever the obstruction is, confront it, explore it, understand and dissolve it. If you do not, and you still create with a strongly focused mind and will, the superimposed outer will must have its effects accordingly. A "willpower construction" conflicts with the inner denial and obstruction. The inability to meditate and create is meaningful and should be heeded, for it will reveal the nature of the obstruction so that you can eliminate it. Otherwise you create willfully on an ego level, which cannot satisfy your heart and soul.

The ego-mind has the power to create. It does so continually. But if it creates separately from the inner being, the results must be disappointing. Willpower, the outer will, can indeed be effective up to a certain degree. It creates matter, sub-matter and experience, but not to your blessing. It creates with a willfulness that lacks wisdom, understanding, vision and depth. It lacks inner connectedness and wholeness, so that what it constructs is often more painful than desirable. In the example we have chosen, this would manifest in creating a partnership in which those areas in the self that have been neglected would color and affect the relationship, poisoning it as if from underground.

When you find your inner voice resisting the creative thought process, this should be a sign that there are steps to take in self-exploration. You must shift the focus of creation to exploring the meaning of your reluctance to create what you long for.

The Patience of Creation

A second important aspect about re-creation is the time element that you, on the ego level, have to deal with. Impatience is another distortion from a fuller state of consciousness, in which creation is immediate. The thought produces the form the moment it is uttered. Impatience is the memory of this experience, without the connectedness with the inner being, so that the lesson the ego has to learn is not comprehended. Only on the ego level is everything separate: effect from cause, soul from soul, form and experience from thought, inner from outer. Life itself appears to you a static, "objective" fixed thing into which you are put. It seems totally separated and disconnected from your inner processes. These are the same illusions as your concept and experience of time, distance, and movement. They are all by-products of the limited, separated ego state. Everything you experience seems to exist only in those seemingly objective terms of the ego. The more you focus in that direction, the more it will seem that way to you. In reality, your life is merely a subjective expression of yourself, not a fixed, objective, immovable reality.   Once you learn to be more focused into the inner reality, you will perceive much more this other, fuller reality, in which the separated aspects move together in a wonderful and meaningful web of interaction and wholeness.

Part of the creating process is the patience to let things be, learning to trust life to express back to you what you put into it. That requires waiting for the seed to grow. Do you wait in doubt? Do you wait with impatience? Do you wait in fear? Do you wait in tension? Do you want whatever it is so badly that you create a forcing current which prohibits fulfillment because its tension and its emotional mind-content defeat creation? If the waiting is truly relaxed, you will have no doubts about the fulfillment.

The re-creating process unfolds forevermore when the ego personality unites with the other aspects of self that had previously not manifested on the surface. The more this happens, the more joyfully you will create. It may sound confusing when I say that you have to learn not to cringe from pain, and then say that it is your birthright to be in a state of joy. It may sound like a contradiction when I say you have to be willing to give-up —at least for the moment, and in the right spirit —what you wish to create and that you must have faith in being able to create. But these are contradictions only on the most superficial ego level where the duality of either/or reigns supreme. In reality these are mutually interdependent principles that must unite in harmony. As you cramp yourself into any desire that is too strong, you close the doors to joy and relaxed inner creation. Cramp always indicates negation, doubt, a negativity that you must unearth and specifically deal with.

In the delusion of the ego, you perceive life as your enemy, foreign and antagonistic to you, while you are its victim. In that delusion you cannot create. So you will see, my friends, that your realization on this path of how you create your suffering will inevitably free you to create your happiness.

Let me close by saying that you are a great deal more than you can possibly believe now. If you walk in the direction of finding your real self, of identifying with it through the layers of darkness, you must discover the unending beauty of the universe. With every breath you take you fill yourself with its potent love and wisdom. There is nothing that surrounds and permeates you that does not express the magnitude of a divine and benign creation. The more aware you become of it, the more joy and gratefulness must spread in your heart. The unending beauty of the universe can be experienced as reality rather than theory only when you work your way through your dark areas.

Be blessed, every one of you. Feel the love that is extended to you from a realm in which you have many friends who have guided you here. Be in peace.

CHAPTER 18

The Cosmic Feeling

Blessings and help are given to you. Love and strength are pouring forth. The divine kernel is in every one of you. The aim of living is to realize this, to know who you really are, to remember. Once you know your true self, which is divine heritage, you will no longer fear or suffer. The work in which I guide you helps, by its various approaches, to eliminate the obstacles to finding out who you are.

These are mere words for most human beings; only after you have overcome certain obstacles can you occasionally experience your true identity. In this lecture I should like to discuss one of the experiences you may have when you begin to glimpse your true identity. I want to prepare you to understand the meaning of this experience so that you do not reject its magnificence by trying to fit it into the mold of the usual human experience —that would destroy it and make its recurrence more difficult. The purpose of this lecture is also to help you attain your true identity sooner and to eliminate the purely mental obstacles.

I wish to discuss a very specific feeling, a feeling that is rarely recognized because it transcends the human being's usual experience of feelings. The feeling I wish to discuss is beyond love. It is generally a very rare human experience, except to the few people who reach full self-realization.

The feeling I am describing might be called, for lack of a better name, *the cosmic feeling*. This cosmic feeling is not merely a theoretical understanding, or a feeling about the cosmos or creation. It is a physical, mental, emotional, and spiritual experience. It encompasses the entire person. I shall try to describe this experience as best I can within the limitations of human language. Then I shall explain the prerequisites for attaining this cosmic feeling, the four keys which make it possible.

An Experience of Unity

The cosmic feeling is an experience in which feeling and thinking are no longer split. It is feeling and thinking in one. This is hard to imagine when one has never had such an experience. But some of you have occasionally experienced the oneness of feeling and thinking. It is an experience of bliss, of the comprehension of life and its mysteries; of all-encompassing love; of the knowledge that all is well and there is nothing to fear. The total absence of fear is something that is very hard for the average person to imagine, partly because you are so unaware of your fears and partly because you are so used to living with them that it does not occur to you that life could be otherwise. Fearless love and joy is a feeling-experience that transcends your little, personal self. It includes everything — and you feel the oneness of all in the universe.

Your usual failure to distinguish between what is real and what is false creates apparently endless confusion and pain. While you believe in illusions, you usually reverse the true order of the universe: You think that what is real is nonexistent. But knowing what is real and what is illusion is part of the experience of the cosmic feeling. This experience lends an immense security, a knowledge of being truly safe, which in turn releases much energy that is felt as bliss in every part of your being. You then experience relaxation and excitement, peace and pleasure as interconnected aspects, rather than mutually exclusive opposites, as you ordinarily experience them. This oneness contains every particle of your body, soul, spirit.

Needless to say that in this state no worry or anxiety can possibly exist. Nor is there a tight pulling within to drive you and make you restless. Restlessness is an expression of the inner urge to seek the path of truth toward full self-realization, but before you have found it the drive can be painful and can make you search temporarily in the wrong direction, leading you even further away from what your innermost self seeks. The pull may be subtle or strongly noticeable. It has its function, but it uses energy that will later be available for the blissful knowing-feeling of the presence of God within. The immediacy of this incredibly powerful presence is at first shocking. The good feeling is shocking. Therefore, the ego must grow sufficiently strong and healthy to bear the high vibrations when the inner presence of God emanates into the outer person. This presence is then experienced as your eternal reality and state—

your true identity. The moment you find yourself in this state, you will know in a most profound way that you have always known what you now rediscover, that you have always been what you now experience yourself to be —that none of this is really new. You had only temporarily cut yourself off from this state of feeling and knowing, of experiencing life as it really is. The experience becomes possible the moment you can bear the immediacy of your divine kernel's presence, its consciousness, its energy, its sparkling reality, its all-permeating wisdom, its all-inclusive love, its creative power that is yours to use as you see fit.

Four Keys to the Cosmic Feeling

Now I shall discuss the four keys or prerequisites for becoming strong enough to bear the power that you hold, and the wisdom embedded in you, and the love hidden inside you, ready to flow out. Every one of you, without exception—every living thing in the universe, —is permeated with this power and intelligence; all that varies is the degree to which the power and the intelligence become manifest.

The four keys are aspects of the pathwork. But they must also be seen in the context of the cosmic feeling. They follow.

1. Understanding Personal Cause and Effect: Understanding cause and effect in your life is essential for self-realization, for the realization of your divine identity. It is essential merely for good health, for being centered within and reasonably integrated, for meaningful functioning and satisfying experiences. *The moment you can see the level in you where your concepts, intentions, and attitudes create your life circumstances, you have your key to create a different and more desirable life.* But when you are disconnected from the creating power in you, when you create unconsciously, you are ignorant of your own power, and you get involved in a chain reaction of error and distortion. You are then in a state where you constantly make others—people, circumstances, life as a whole—responsible for your misery. This brings further chain reactions. This inner state —whether you are conscious of it or not—makes you blame, accuse, and feel victimized. In turn you feel justified to hate, resent, and take revenge.

Salvation can come only when you realize your beautiful birthright to create. Just as you create negatively, so can you create positively. Just as you create willfully from the little ego, following the dictates of vanity, greed, laziness, and dishonesty, so can you create by letting God express in you and create honestly and beautifully.

You are fortunate that the progress of your self-work has brought many of you in contact with the level of your negative creation. You begin to see more clearly which attitudes, expressions, and intentionalities have produced manifestations in your life that you deplore and have complained about while passively waiting for some miracle to happen from outside —or in the face of which you have given up and adjusted to unnecessary deprivation and frustration. There is still much work to be done by each of you in searching out your negative self-creation. There are still many areas of your lives you gloss over and fail to give the scrutiny so essential for this discovery.

When you can truly connect with your creative level, you will find such relief; you will find the world opening up. It will dawn on you that if you can create unconsciously, inadvertently, and erroneously such tangible events and states of mind; you can also create consciously, deliberately, and intentionally the circumstances and the state of mind that you desire.

For example, if you now become aware that you cannot bear full happiness and pleasure—if the current is too strong and disquieting—you can create this capacity in yourself by stating the desire and intent, by being willing to give up your dishonesty and negative intentionality, and by wanting to give honestly the best that is in you. How else can you find the endless wealth that is in you? By holding back your inner giving, your openness, and your commitment to life, you increase your sense of inner poverty, your belief that you are empty and have nothing to give. The one who feels empty gives nothing. You can feel rich and full only when you wish to give. The moment you do this you create positively, and you will gradually see your creations grow. They may sometimes take a few years to fully manifest, sometimes less. They are never completed. Positive creations can be endlessly enlarged. By truly seeing the cause and effect of your negative creation and its manifestations, you become a creator. You realize your birthright of divinity.

2. Feeling All Your Feelings: It requires some growing and groping before the personality can accept all feelings, experiencing and handling them constructively. I have said much about how to do this, so now I will discuss this topic only as it relates to the cosmic feeling.

If humankind goes through the depths of unhappy, painful feelings, it is because it has created them and can grow beyond them only by going through them. Many of you have already experienced the truth that by fully accepting and feeling your pain, you become commensurately capable of sustaining pleasure. By humbly and honestly admitting your hate and expressing it constructively, that is, assuming responsibility for it, your capacity to love grows commensurately. By willingly experiencing your fear, you grow fearless and secure. This is so because the apparently opposite feelings are one and the same energy current, appearing in different frequencies and degrees of condensation. The vibration changes as you discover the oneness of the opposites. The more you avoid a feeling, the less you can experience its other side.

The cosmic feeling is of the highest frequency of energy. If any other feeling within the ordinary human spectrum is still apparently unmanageable, cosmic feeling is much too strong to bear.

As long as you shy away from a feeling, it remains a wall, it remains your enemy, and you must remain frightened of your own feelings. By that dynamic you create the twice-removed alienation process that is so disconcerting and painful: Fear of your fear; pain about your pain; hate for your hate. Your inner split widens until you start groping your way back.

There is no feeling in existence, no matter what it is, that cannot be fully experienced and dealt with in a constructive, beautiful way. If you air out your most negative feelings —hate, cruelty, anger, and rage, and their by-products of envy, jealousy, greed, dishonesty, and so on —their clean and honest expression is beautiful. It is beautiful because you no longer pretend; you risk being truthful and thus become beautiful as you expose the ugliness. If you have the courage and trust in the universe to truly expose a negative part of your consciousness and if you ask for inner guidance to help you in this endeavor, you will experience the powerful energy contained in the previously hidden feelings. This energy is absolutely essential for creating your life, for expanding your life and consciousness, for feeling joy and pleasure. Tiredness, listlessness, lack of energy can be explained by many outer factors, but in the last analysis they are always products of running away from feeling and thus of repressing your vital energy.

There is no pain that, if you meet it constructively and with out false ideas and projections, will not prove to be a tunnel through which you go comparatively quickly, releasing beautiful energy, love, and power. There is no hate so ugly, or nega tive intentionality so awful, that expressing it honestly —rather than acting it out against others —will not yield powerful energy and add to the beauty of your love and your environment. No hate, no pain, no fear is ever permanent, but love, pleasure, security, peace, and bliss are permanent conditions. Hate, pain, fear are but frozen energy, distorted consciousness. Every time you feel reluctant to go into a pain or into your rage, it is only dishonesty that makes you reluctant — the wish to appear different from the way you really are. When you overcome your imagined need to pretend, when you can be who you are, there is no feeling that cannot be a source of creative energy. Being honest includes challenging your conscious or unconscious assumption that if you go into pain, you will become lost in it and perish.

By the same token, only when you can accept and sustain ordinary good feelings can your ability to sustain the cosmic feeling grow. It is important to understand this evolutionary process of your feeling nature; it will explain why you are so often incapable of holding on to good feelings. You see yourself contract again, right after you have opened up and experienced pleasure, love, the goodness of life. You know that this principle exists, but you still do not use it enough for the gauge that it is; it points to unrecognized, unaccepted, unexpressed negative feelings. And if occasionally a glimmer of the cosmic feeling comes and quickly slips away, it is a sign that your love capacity is not as developed as it can and will be. The strongest human love experience is only a lukewarm, mild shadow of the cosmic feeling that encompasses everything.

3. Developing Positive Intentionality: You must develop positive intentionality not superficially, not just to comply with some rules, but from the core of your real being, where you want truth and love for their own sakes rather than for what you wish to gain. It must exist on that deep level where you keep discovering the dishonesty and negative intentions toward life, which are the true causes of your unhappiness. The moment you can risk looking at your negative intentions and begin to really work with them on this deep level, your positive intentionality will express itself strongly. Then there will be love—love for the universe, love for yourself, love for others, love for creation. Your love lacks totality to the degree that negative intentionality festers in your psyche. And you cannot have cosmic feeling unless you have love.

The commitment to make a fair exchange with life must be made over and over day in and day out, searching for deeper hidden recesses where negative intentionality may still exist and then reversing it in a deliberate, creative act of expressing positive intentionality.

How can you gauge where hidden negative intentionality exists? You can gauge it easily by simply asking, "Where am I still unhappy? Where am I anxious? Where do I have problems with myself, with life, with others?" No matter how easy it may be to ascribe the cause to others, there is nevertheless something in you that you do not see. Your own unhappiness is your gauge, and you can use it every day. Nothing could be more reliable. In your daily review each night, ask yourself, "Is my life as fulfilled, as joyful, as rich and meaningful as I long for it to be?" Then you have your answer, and you can explore yourself further by asking, "What do I contribute to this situation? How do I create it?"

Even if your life is fulfilled and happy, and you see it become increasingly richer, you can still ask yourself, "Which are the areas in my life where I still feel flat and where I do not feel the joy that I know otherwise to exist?" It is really very simple to do this, my friends, and once you focus in this way, you will see it as simple as a diagram you can draw with the simplest stroke. It is truly no mystery.

4. Developing the Capacity to Connect with Your Innermost Divine Nucleus: The other three points are surely prerequisites to this. The fourth point cannot truly be used successfully unless the other three have been put into practice. The fourth key is meditational. Listen into yourself, become calm and receptive, quiet the busy, loud mind. Start with the premise that there is a deep nucleus of knowing, feeling, power, and presence within you. Focus on it lightly, without the feeling that "I must experience it now." Wait calmly. Learn to become inwardly relaxed. See your own inner rushing, driving, grasping. Observe it, until you can stop it. It may at first be a pain, but this is then an opportunity to feel the pain without resistance. Learn the great art of tuning in. Ask your innermost Godself for help in this. Persevere. Give your attention and your good will to the practice. One day the channel will open. Contemplate the possibility that there are faculties within you that you have not yet experienced.

There is an inner ear with which you will eventually hear; an inner eye with which you will see; an inner power with which you will perceive. These faculties are not yet in use, but they can be awakened. As you put to rest your thoughts and your doubts, which are a trick of the ego, and as you increase your capacity to see through the ego's tricks and be attentive to your inner movements, again and again asking for inner guidance, you will awaken and develop a new inner faculty. It may appear in different realms for different people. With one, the inner ear will suddenly open and you will hear God in you. You will know it is not imagination—nothing could be more real. With another, the inner eye will begin to see —perhaps symbolic forms or pictures. It may see on an inner level, where seeing is knowing. It may see the light of truth and of love. That seeing will become understanding, for understanding must always follow to integrate the experience with the conscious ego personality. Still another may discover an ability to express the inner knowing in thoughts: "It" thinks in you, instructs you, or perhaps writes through you. There are many different ways in which new knowing, new seeing, new hearing, new experiencing come from the divine kernel within.

Everyone can be helped by this lecture to understand where he or she is on the path, regardless of whether each person can actually put everything to use at this point. That may come only later.

If you truly surrender to God's will and guidance, wonderful things will happen. Allow them to happen. Enrich yourself and do not shy away from the risk and from the momentary resistance. Do not cut yourself off from it. Be blessed, my dear ones!

CHAPTER 19

Jesus Christ
and Courage

Joyfully I bring divine blessings that can touch everyone here in a very vital way. You need to raise your consciousness to this reality. You need to remove the barriers that prevent you from perceiving God's presence and love in your life.

It is the ultimate aim of self-realization to establish the truth of God, of eternal life, of the benign meaning of everything in every crevice of consciousness. This process is the very reason for incarnation and purification. What do you think purification is all about? It is not just to become "good." Absolute good can be found only on the most profound levels of truth. The greatest truth of God's reality and immediacy brings you to the ultimate good that is beyond all question and doubt.

Even though you have strengthened your faith and your realization that this world is infused with God, few have as yet made personal contact. God became human so as to always be close to you in a very personal, loving way. For most believers God is a much less personal, more vague and general experience. And you know that you can experience only that which you can conceive of and believe in.

If you seriously long, pray, and search for a realization of Jesus Christ's personal love for you, the answers will come forth. Perhaps you will not recognize the first answers as such. They may have something to do with specific barriers that prevent you from experiencing this reality. They may bring up new, or again old, material on your path that you need to work on for your purification. These are the answers! Once the barriers begin to crumble, you will experience what it means to *feel* Jesus Christ's personal love for you.

Total Surrender to the Will of God
You need the wisdom to comprehend that the highest, most desirable, most unified state of consciousness, the ultimate of all

fulfillment that includes and encompasses and transcends all other desirable states and attainments, cannot come quickly, cheaply, easily. By this I mean that your total focus, commitment, devotion must be generated and activated by your active mind and will. Your total goal in life must be to find the reality of the living God as immediate experience. Not as theoretical speculation and a luxury of belief, but as living reality in your inner and outer life.

As you thus proceed on your path, the glory that will come to you cannot be put into words. However, this total fulfillment can come only as you totally surrender to the will of God, without any reservations, in every large and small aspect of your life and your being. How difficult this remains for most of you. You keep holding back. You still have your little corners of holding out, of believing that your selfwill knows better than God what makes you happy. Yet Jesus Christ is here to give you eternal life, safety and total fulfillment, if only you trust Him and give yourself to Him. You will be sustained with all the juices of life and joy in a constant flow of renewal.

You cannot eliminate your fears and your distrust of others unless you constantly renew the practice of total surrender to the highest within yourself. For you cannot subsist alone. No creature can. All created beings hang together on a chain of interdependence—physically, emotionally and spiritually. When the weight of dependence is put where it belongs —on God, on God's personalized aspect who is personally near you— then you can create a healthy center of gravity anchored deep within your soul, for that is where to find Him. His presence merges with your higher self. You truly become one.

So, my beloved friends, make it your business now to deepen your desire for personal contact with Christ. Strengthen your commitment to Him, to give over all of your life to Him in the total trust that He deserves. Your human fears can never be assuaged otherwise.

Salvation

Let us speak about salvation. The traditional interpretation of this word leaves a lot to be desired. It lends itself easily to misunderstanding, although the more enlightened among religionists do perceive the truth. Salvation means, among other things, Christ's endless forgiveness and acceptance. It means that you can always find your way to God, no matter what you have done, no matter what your lower self still wishes to do.

The door is always open. You are never, never locked out.

All you have to do is knock. Ask for the bread of God's mercy, love, forgiveness and personal help in all ways, and you shall not receive a stone. Ask to know yourself, your lovability, your nobility of spirit, the beauty of your true being, through His redemptive love of you, and you shall receive it. That is salvation. All that— and more. God's personalized aspect has brought it about. The incarnated Christ has made it possible for all other incarnated entities to be saved from their painful state of untruth— sin— and consequent destructiveness of self and others.

Let us now discuss three interdependent aspects of salvation that create much confusion and contradiction among humankind. I am speaking here specifically of the salvation of your personal soul. There are other aspects of salvation which go beyond that. They have to do with the possibility of every created entity leaving behind the state of consciousness that might be called hell —or various lesser stages of it: states of consciousness that reflect error and therefore suffering, the wheel of death and rebirth which carries with it fears due to a break in consciousness.

Christ's demonstration of supreme love, forgiveness and mercy —of acceptance due to the deep penetration of His vision into our ultimate nature—opened all doors that were closed before. They were closed, not because God punished humankind and therefore locked the doors, but because humans were deeply immersed in the conviction that they could not be forgiven and that they were therefore doomed to suffer eternally. This, in turn, took away all the incentive to work on any process of self-purification. Where there is no hope, will and incentive are also lacking. Through the life and death of Jesus a new modality was created within the human mind. This new model enabled human beings to choose the path the Master showed. He has said that He is the way, He is truth, He is life. It was no longer futile to try. Forgiveness for every transgression exists already, because God recognizes in much deeper terms why you are driven as you are, why you must go through your sins in order to recognize them for what they are, so that a new incentive spurs you on to the great journey you are now undertaking.

The personal aspect of salvation seems confusing to the mind that is steeped in the dualism of either/or. Let me present these three paradoxical aspects:

1. Only you yourself can effect your salvation. It is your responsibility.

2. You cannot possibly do it alone. You need the help of others who share the journey with you, who may often see what you do not see.

3. Without God, without the personal assistance of the personal aspect of God, the undertaking is too vast for you to accomplish.

These three may no longer seem contradictory or confusing to those of you who have worked for a time with my lectures about duality and the unitive principle. You may see quite clearly that these categories are not mutually exclusive. Yet some among you may still feel a confusion and ask, "How could it be that, although I am solely responsible to do it myself, I need others, as well as God?" Even for those who are not particularly confused about this concept of salvation it may be helpful to have more clarity on the subject.

Yes, it is obviously true that your salvation is your choice, your intent, your responsibility, your will, your effort—and often what seems to be your sacrifice. At least it seems a sacrifice at first to give up time and energy for the undertaking of your self-work. It often seems even more of a sacrifice to shed a habit that stems from your lower self and gives you some lower-self gratifications for a while, so that higher pleasures can take root in you. No one else, not even the Creator, can make you do what you do not wish and choose to do. This would go directly against all spiritual law whose author, after all, is God.

Yet you are often too involved in your misperceptions of your reality and too blind about your role in your interaction with others to be able to set distorted perceptions right. You need the mirror of others. You need to learn to be open to them. You need to learn to give up your pretenses, and therefore your defenses, in your relationship with them. You need to show yourself as you are, with all your vulnerability and total inner truth. This in itself is already an integral part of your journey toward self-realization. You need to learn to receive, even though this may first make you feel weak and vulnerable, for only then can you give of yourself. Working with others, being open to and with them, fulfills the law of brotherhood.

As for point three, how could you learn to love yourself without at least knowing, and finally experiencing, God's love for you? How could you activate the power to change involuntary aspects that do not directly respond to your outer will? The outer will and the outer aspects that respond to it need to be activated aggressively by your dedication to your path, by the many daily decisions to face the truth in difficult or confusing situations, by your choice to fulfill the law of brotherhood and overcome your initial resistance to showing yourself as you are. But then comes a point in which you deal with involuntary emotions, responses, reactions and even beliefs that do not respond, no matter how sincerely your outer self wants to change them. So you constantly need the higher powers to help you find the way into those deeper levels and effect a change that your own mind alone cannot bring about.

All this also teaches you the wisdom to distinguish between where the self is the master and where you desperately need the Great Master without whom nothing can be accomplished.

The surrender of your will to God's will and the dedication of your life, your talents, and attributes to the great plan not only make you flourish in your daily life but are the key to the unification of your split, where you are still torn between belief and unbelief, trust and fear, hate and love, ignorance and wisdom, separateness and union, death and eternal life.

The Spiritual Are Courageous

One of the most important attributes in this struggle is courage. The role of courage is often underestimated. In fact, most people assume that spiritual people are weak and meek, implying that they are without courage, for courage requires strength and energy. The spineless are often assumed to be victims of the aggressive, bold ones. Thus, on some irrational level of your emotional perception, courage is often associated with evil, while the weak, timid person is associated with mildness, gentleness, goodness. Nothing could be further from the truth. Spiritual cowardice not only leads to betrayal of the best, of God, but to evil that is as active and potent as the more obvious aggressive acting out of cruel, self-serving, dishonest malice. It is important to be fully aware of this, to liberate yourself from the illusion that your weakness, your timidity, are really not so harmful, and perhaps are even more spiritual than the fighting spirit of those who risk themselves and their personal advantages by aggressive goodness and positive assertion.

What happens when you are weak, when you do not stand up to evil behavior, when you collude with it and refrain from fighting for the truth? You encourage evil, you sustain the illusion in the person who perpetrates it that it is not so bad, that it is all right, that it is smart and that many people support it. This perpetuates the further illusion that by asserting truth, standing up for decency, and exposing evil, you will be isolated, ridiculed, and rejected. In other words, you foster the delusion that in order to be accepted one needs to sell out integrity and decency.

All this happens constantly in human interaction. Such encouragement of evil is easy to push out of full awareness. Yet around the person who indulges in this kind of negative behavior there is a cloud of guilt, confusion, and an emotional climate of self-rejection. No matter how you try to talk yourself out of self-hate and into self-esteem on theoretical grounds, you will not succeed until you have gained the spiritual courage to be willing to sacrifice acceptance from others —if indeed you believe that this price has to be paid.

When someone in your presence maligns another, for example, your silence is not goodness, gentleness, peacefulness. Far from it. In a sense it is more destructive and insidiously negative than outright, active maligning. Maligners expose their evil and thus take the chance of being rebuked and having to face the consequences. Passive listeners cheat by trying to have it both ways: They derive as much negative gratification from the maligning as the active one, without risking any negative consequences, and even priding themselves that they really did not participate in the act.

Active evil alone could never have led to the crucifixion of Jesus. It required the cooperation of the traitors, the colluders, the silent bystanders who were afraid for their skin and thus allowed evil to—apparently—win. But, of course, evil can never really win.

The same is true of the mass murders in totalitarian regimes, such as in Germany before and during the last war. The few perpetrators could not have gotten very far if they had not been aided by the silent collusion of the many for whom their own skin was more important than truth, decency, honesty, charity, love, empathy —in short, all that God stands for.

This leads to an interesting speculation, my friends; namely, that the active principle in distortion, harmful and murderous as it may be, could never by itself wreak the same havoc as the passive, receptive principle in distortion. This is why many spiritual teachings say that the lowest quality on the whole scale is not hatred, but inertia. Inertia, on the energy level, is the freezing of the flow of divine energy. In inertia the radiant matter of divine influx thickens, hardens, blocks, and deadens. On the level of consciousness, inertia means exactly what I have been talking about. It includes primary and secondary guilt. The primary guilt is for cooperation with evil, permitting it, conveying one's approval of it, no matter how subtly and indirectly. The secondary guilt lies in pretending and claiming that one is not participating in the evil, and even pretending to be good, while one's cowardice and self-serving gives silent permission to the evil act. This is why Jesus Christ, in his life on earth, always stressed that the evil-doer is nearer to God than the self-righteous, pretending-to-be-good person.

Stagnation and inertia are indeed the greatest evil. They are of matter, resisting the enlivening power of the spirit, of the eternal, which desires to penetrate the void. False receptivity is masked inertia. The more false receptivity exists, the less real receptivity is possible. The inability to receive love, pleasure, and fulfillment, and the compulsion to sabotage fulfillment come from not giving to God. When you give to God, you need to be active, to overcome inertia, to move and do and act, to risk and sometimes to fight against your own and others' evil. Only then will you feel free from guilt and become truly receptive to what the universe wants to give to you. The grace of God is everywhere around and within you. It is always there; you are bathed in it.

Giving to God means to give over to the great plan, to God's will, and to dedicate your life to this. Giving to God means activity, and at times even pushing through the inertia that wants to keep you from being active. The activity may be directed to many areas, apart from fighting the obvious resistance to your growth process. Such movement is necessary in the smallest details of daily living when you are involved in the noble process of creating a new society. You may have to deal actively with apparently menial, mundane issues. You may have to confront actively the resistance to changes that are so necessary to the process of being and living according to the principles of divine law. So, my friends, ascertain the exact nature of your inertia, and, even more important, how you rationalize it in order to indulge in it.

When you still feel weak, confused, self-rejecting, or unful-filled in any area, when you are divided within yourself and fluctuate between submission and rebellion, you know quite well that you are divided. You are not yet autonomous. The only way true autonomy can be established is by your total sur-render to the will of God. This must include the willingness to be temporarily hurt, rejected, or put at a disadvantage. It must include the courage to risk something or to sacrifice a selfish aim. It also includes the faith that this is truly in your own best interest, even from a very human point of view.

Your primary attitude in life must become dedication to God's will and plan, your giving over in all things and putting God first. All other things then become the natural effects of this attitude and will be fulfilled accordingly. Perhaps you now put emphasis on your profession, your mate, your personal ful-fillment, rather than letting these other fulfillments flow as a natural byproduct of your dedication to your task for God, the task you are meant to carry out as part of the great army fight-ing for the forces of good. Meditate on these vast issues that fill your universe and are of utmost importance in the scheme of all things: the great battle between the forces of good and the forces of evil engaged in the gradual penetration of life into the void. When you perceive this vast, universal issue as the key to all other issues, you will begin to put first things first and see your private world in its proper perspective. This will bring a wonderful new balance and harmony into your life and lead you directly to the faith, the knowledge of the ever-living God and of your individual immortality that alone can still the deep existential longing.

With this I bless you, my most beloved friends. Let this blessing open your whole being, your heart, and your mind. Experience the Creator in whom you live all the time. Experience the utter safety and joy, the limitless fountain of creative possibilities that this entails. Give to your life a one-pointed direction to fulfill yourself. This can be done only with and through God.

Glossary

Daily Review

The daily review is a practice to develop self-knowledge. The lectures suggest that every day we jot down moments of negative, disharmonious feelings, such as fear, indignation, anger, overreaction, or feeling victimized. In unconsciousness, we believe that the events causing such feelings come to us unbidden. However, reviewing our notes after several weeks, we are surprised to find how repetitious they are. This clearly indicates our active participation in these events, even in provoking them. We then see that we are not victims in the sense we had thought. Perhaps we are victims of our own unconsciousness! Seeing the patterns will lead us to search and find the underlying emotional stance that is constantly creating the same situations. The daily review is therefore extremely important in indicating the elements of the images, our firmly held misconceptions, so that we can recognize and deactivate them.

It is also useful to write down, in another part of the notebook, messages from our higher self, or inspirational words that have touched us, to help us avoid the error of identifying ourselves with the distorted parts that create disharmony.

Helper

A helper is a Pathwork practitioner, someone deeply involved in the purification work according to the Pathwork teachings, trained to help others in their development. Helpers give one-to-one sessions, lead groups, teach the Pathwork. Helpers continue their own growth by continuing to have sessions with another Pathwork helper. Helpers are required to go through a period of supervised helpership.

The Higher Self, the Lower Self, and the Mask

In an effort to represent human nature in its completeness, we can conceive of it in the shape of three concentric spheres. The outer sphere we call the mask self. This we fashion according to how we want others to see us, and how we would like to believe we are. The mask self is also a protection against what we don't want others to see and what we don't want to see within ourselves. In the sense that we want to impress others with it, the mask self is an aspect of what we call the ego. It is a controlled and manipulated expression of ourselves, created for the purpose of attaining some of our hidden and partly unconscious goals.

In creating the mask self, we work — mostly unconsciously, of course — like a sculptor with a model. The model which we try to copy when we make our mask is the idealized self-image. It is a conception of what we want to be, not in the deeply satisfying spiritual sense, but in the sense of meeting the expectations of others and of trying to escape from our own fears. Thus, the idealized self-image contains many harmful misconceptions of which we are unaware. Nevertheless, it has a strongly negative power and controls our lives through the mask self.

Behind the mask self hides the second sphere, that hidden world of egocentricity which we call the lower self. This is actually what the mask self covers up, because we do not want to display or face the fear, the hate, the stinginess, the cruelty, the distorted perceptions, and the intellectual misconceptions of the lower self. It is in the lower self that images have their seat and give rise to negative reactions and patterns which create conflict and misery in our lives.

We all have a higher self, which is the innermost core of our nature. This higher self is part of the universal intelligence and universal love that pervades all life. It is our divine spark. This higher self is free, spontaneous, loving, giving, all-knowing, and capable of uninterrupted joy and bliss. It is the brief contacts with this higher self that give humans their true happiness, their creativity, and their real pleasure. We can get in touch with our higher self through being in truth, giving from our heart and not for personal gain or reward, through caring for and loving each other, and through meditation and prayer.

Images

We are not born with a clear, undistorted perception of reality. Due to previous incarnations and childhood circumstances in this life, we see many situations in a distorted way. When these distortions develop into a firmly-held conclusion about life, we speak of an image. An image is made up of misconceptions, distorted feelings, and physical blocks. Of course, a conclusion drawn from distorted perception is a wrong conclusion; therefore images are actually wrong conclusions about the nature of reality which are so firmly embedded in a person's psyche that they become behavior-controlling signals in life situations. An image of this kind is not subjected to rational examination, but is often defended by elaborate rationalizations.

An example of an image formed under childhood conditioning might be that the display of emotion, especially of warm feelings, is a sign of weakness and will lead to one's being hurt. Although this is a personal image, it may be reinforced by the societal mass image that, especially for a man, the display and physical expression of warm feelings is unmanly and weak because it means losing control. An individual with this image will then, in any situation where he could emotionally open himself, obey the signal of the images instead of spontaneously responding to the actual situation or person, which would be the positive, life-affirming response. He also acts toward others in such a way that they will respond negatively to him and confirm his false belief. Thus he deprives himself of pleasure and restricts the flow of the life force, creating inner tensions and further feeding his image. The effect of such images on the individual is the creating of negative compulsive patterns and reactions that restrict the unfolding of his potential.

The Life Force

The Life Force is the free-flowing energy current manifest in the universe in all beings, things, and ideas. Nothing exists without it. The life force has three essential aspects: movement, consciousness, and experience.

When we do not resist the life force which is always flowing through us, we can experience bliss. This becomes possible when our entire organism is in harmony with reality on the physical, emotional, mental, and spiritual levels. This means giving up misconceptions and defenses which prevent integration of the personality with the life force. To make this possible we must be in movement, allow ourselves to grow, attain a consciousness beyond duality, and experience all feelings deeply without resistance.

Even in our present state of being we can contact the life force when we clarify the confusion of distorted feelings, thoughts, and moods. When we accept the truth of the present state and are willing to be in the now, we will immediately become imbued with the wisdom and joy of the life force. As our development continues, the life force is experienced not only in rare moments, but becomes a part of our life.

Negative Intentionality and Positive Intentionality

Negative intentionality is that part of the self which is locked into negation. It is not the same as negativity. Negativity comprises a wide range of feelings such as envy, hate, fear, or pride. Negative intentionality is deliberate choice to hold on to a state of negating life and the self. It is also a means of punishing life. Courage and humility are required to recognize that there is such a spot of ill will inside us. There is a twisted, immature reasoning behind this attitude and behind the resistance to give it up. If these are recognized, the road is open to the transition to positive intentionality, and thus to liberation.

To move into the attitude of positive intentionality you need to cultivate a deep inner certainty that the abundance and creative power of the universe transcends every limitation. You can create a positive attitude toward life according to a lawful, integrative process of transformation that makes you totally self-responsible. To make it work you need to adopt a trusting attitude toward yourself and life. Anchored in your good will, knowing that the power is yours, you can expose your negative intentionality. Otherwise it is impossible to transform it. As you become free of your negative intentionality, you are no longer devastated by that of others. You will become open to love, in the awareness that the universe is a rich and joyous place in which you are at home.

Real Self

The Real Self is our higher self seen as our true identity. Spiritual truths can often be expressed only in paradoxes: So defined, the real self is both our actuality and our potentiality. We are already our real selves underneath the layers of confusion, fear, and error. Yet the real self is also the potentially perfect self, the state we attain when these layers have been transformed and eliminated. Our real self lives in unity, having never left that divine state. We call it *real* in contrast to our disconnected aspects that are in illusion.

Unity and Duality

Human beings live in duality. Thus they perceive everything through pairs of opposites: good or evil, light or dark, right or wrong, living or dead. This is so because our consciousness is split. This dualistic way of perceiving conceals from us the deeper reality of the universe, which is fundamental unity. Every soul longs for the unified state of consciousness — a state of absolute reality, bliss, freedom, and fulfillment. It is possible to attain—or at least catch glimpses of this state— for our real self lives in this unified state even when we are unaware of it. We experience it when we identify with our higher selves; then duality is transcended. Once a soul has consciously experienced this state of being even for a second, there is always the possibility to challenge the split dualistic state by remembering one's true nature and the oneness of all life.

Vicious Circle

Psychologically speaking, a vicious circle is a self-perpetuating, repetitive pattern of negative, destructive, illusory attitudes which intensify one another. It originates in an image or misconception which separates us from the reality of a situation; as the vicious circle progresses, we get further and further away from correcting the original mistake. Take, for instance, somebody who has the misconception that the only way to defend himself against being hurt by others is to make them afraid of him. Even if he initially did not elicit hostile feelings, in his endeavor to frighten others he will certainly evoke them. This hostility will make him more threatening and tyrannical and he will use all new evidence to reconfirm his original misconception. Finally he is bound to have some unpleasant experience, which he will interpret as the result of his not having been "strong enough." Thus he remains a prisoner of his vicious circle and goes through the same experience again and again.

Textual Note

Each chapter in this book is an edited version of a Pathwork lecture or lectures. Since chapter titles are not always the same as the original titles of the lectures, we give here a listing of chapter numbers and the equivalent lecture numbers.

Chapter 1 is a blend of lecture #10 and lecture #211.

Chapter 2 is lecture #3.

Chapter 3 is lecture #5.

Chapter 4 is lecture #52 plus a few pages written by Eva Pierrakos.

Chapter 5 is lecture #105.

Chapter 6 is lecture #75.

Chapter 7 is lecture #144.

Chapter 8 is lecture #149.

Chapter 9 is lecture #145.

Chapter 10 is lecture #158.

Chapter 11 is lecture #217.

Chapter 12 is lecture #112.

Chapter 13 is lecture #220.

Chapter 14 is lecture #15.

Chapter 15 is lecture #197.

Chapter 16 is lecture #248.

Chapter 17 is lecture #208.

Chapter 18 is lecture #200.

Chapter 19 is the first half of lecture #258 and the second half of lecture #244.

List of
Pathwork Lectures

*The following lectures are available from the Pathwork Centers
listed on pages 203 and 204.*

1. The Sea of Life
2. Decisions and Tests
3. Choosing Your Destiny
4. World Weariness
5. Happiness as a Link in the Chain of Life
6. Man's Place in the Spiritual and Material Universes
7. Asking for Help and Helping Others
8. Contact with God's Spirit World—Mediumship
9. The Lord's Prayer
10. Male and Female Incarnations—Their Rhythm and Causes
11. Know Thyself
12. The Order and Diversity of the Spiritual Worlds—
    The Process of Reincarnation
13. Positive Thinking
14. The Higher Self, the Lower Self, and the Mask
15. Influence Between the Spiritual and Material Worlds
16. Spiritual Nourishment
17. The Call
18. Free Will
19. Jesus Christ
20. God—the Creation
21. The Fall
22. Salvation
25. The Path
26. Finding One's Faults
27. Escape Possible Also on the Path
28. Communication with God
29. Activity and Passivity
30. Self-Will, Pride, and Fear
31. Shame
32. Decision-Making
33. Occupation with Self
34. Preparation for Reincarnation
35. Turning to God
36. Prayer
37. Acceptance—Dignity in Humility
38. Images
39. Image-Finding
40. More on Images

List of Pathwork Centers Worldwide

We welcome the opportunity to support you in connecting with others worldwide who are interested in exploring this material further. To order any Pathwork Lecture or books, or for further information, please contact the following regional centers:

California
Pathwork of California
1355 Stratford Court #16
Del Mar, California 92014
ph (619) 793-1246 fax (619) 259-5224
e-mail: CAPathwork@aol.com

Central United States
Pathwork of Iowa
24 Highland Drive
Iowa City, Iowa 52246
ph (319) 338-9878

Great Lakes Region
Great Lakes Pathwork
1117 Fernwood
Royal Oak, Michigan 48067
ph/fax (248) 585-3984

Mid-Atlantic Region
Sevenoaks Pathwork Center
Route 1, Box 86
Madison, Virginia 22727
ph(540) 948-6544 fax (540)948-3956
e-mail: SevenoaksP@aol.com

New York, New Jersey, New England
Phoenicia Pathwork Center
Box 66
Phoenicia, New York 12464
(800) 201-0036 fax (914)688-2007
e-mail: PATHWORKNY.ORG

Northwest
Northwest Pathwork
811 NW 20th, Suite 103-C
Portland, Oregon 97209
ph(503)223-0018

Philadelphia
Philadelphia Pathwork
901 Bellevue Avenue
Hulmeville, Pennsylvania 19407
ph(215) 752-9894
e-mail: dtilove@itw.com

Southeast
Pathwork of Georgia
120 Blue Pond Court
Canton, Georgia 30115
ph/fax (770) 889-8790

Southwest
Path to the Real Self/Pathwork
Box 3753
Santa Fe, New Mexico 87501
ph (505) 455-2533

You may also call: (800) PATHWORK (728-4967).
Visit the Pathwork website at: http://www.pathwork.org

List of Pathwork Centers Worldwide

(Centers in the United States listed on page 203)

Argentina
Pathwork
Castex 3345, Piso 12, Cap.Fed.
Buenos Aires, Argentina 00541
ph/fax 54-1-801-7024

Brazil Northeast
Conselho do Pathwork
Rua Waldemar Falcao, 377-Brotas
40295-001 Salvador - BA - Brazil
ph 71-334-7151 fax 71-334-2729

Brazil Southeast
Grupos do Pathwork
Rua Roquete Pinto, 401
CEP 05515010
Sao Paulo, SP, Brazil
ph 11-814-4678 fax 11-211-4073

Canada
Ontario/Quebec Pathwork
P.O. Box 164
Pakenham, Ontario KOA-2X0
ph (613) 624-5474

Germany
Pfadgruppe Kiel
Ludemannstrasse 51
24114, Kiel, Germany
ph 0431-66-58-07

Italy
Il Sentiero
Via Campodivivo, 43
04020 Spigno Saturnia (LT)
Italy
ph 39-771-64463 fax 39-771-64693
e-mail: crisalide@fabernet.com
web: http://www.saephir.it./crisalide

Luxembourg
Pathwork Luxembourg
L8274 Brilwee 2
Kehlen, Luxembourg
ph 352-307328

Mexico
Pathwork Mexico
Pino #101, Col Rancho Cortes
Cuernavaca, Mor C.P. 62120
ph 73-131395 fax 73-113592
e-mail: andresle@infosel.net.mx

The Netherlands
Padwerk
Amerikalaan 192
3526 BE Utrecht
The Netherlands
ph/fax 035-6935222
e-mail: Trudi.groos@pi.net

Uruguay
Uruguay Pathwork
Mones Roses 6162
Montevideo 11500, Uruguay
ph 598-2-618612 fax 598-2-920674
e-mail: LGF@adinet.com.uy

The Pathwork Series

The Pathwork of Self-Transformation

by Eva Pierrakos
Edited by Judith Saly

Under such headings as "The Idealized Self-Image," "The Forces of Love, Eros, and Sex," "Emotional Growth and Its Function," "Real and False Needs," and "The Spiritual Meaning of Crisis," the Pathwork outlines the entire process of personal spiritual development. Unlike many overidealized philosophies, the Pathwork confronts our devils as well as our angels, our all-too-human failings and petty ego concerns as well as our divine strengths. It shows us how to accept ourselves fully as we are now, and then to move beyond the negativity, or "lower self," that blocks our personal and spiritual evolution. It offers a practical, rational, and honest way to reach our deepest creative identity.

Bantam, 1990.
ISBN 0-553-34896-5
$12.95

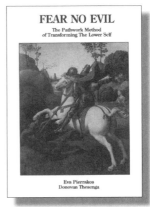

Fear No Evil
The Pathwork Method of Transforming the Lower Self

by Eva Pierrakos
Edited by Donovan Thesenga

Fear No Evil offers a practical method of compassionately observing and transforming our shadow side.

*"**Fear No Evil** can help us face our negative life experiences with a new light of understanding that will transform our personal pain into joy and pleasure."* —*Barbara Brennan*

Pathwork Press, 1993.
ISBN 0-9614777-2-5
$15.95

The Pathwork Series

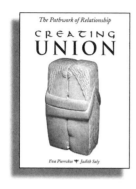

Creating Union
The Pathwork of Relationship
by Eva Pierrakos
Edited by Judith Saly

Creating Union challenges us to courageously undertake the greatest adventure of life, the journey into fearless loving and self-realization with a kindred spirit. ***Creating Union*** provides deep insight into the meaning of our inevitable relationship difficulties and guides us in resolving them to achieve vibrant partnerships. It compassionately answers practical questions about sexuality and spirituality, divorce, intimacy, mutuality and how to keep passion alive.

Pathwork Press, 1993.
ISBN 0-9614777-3-3
$14.95

The Undefended Self
Living the Pathwork of Spiritual Wholeness
by Susan Thesenga

The Undefended Self outlines the Pathwork process of personal transformation and includes true stories of people turning life-long problems into occasions for positive movement and growth.

"I highly recommend *The Undefended Self* for those people who are seriously interested in the deeper levels of self and its transformation. **This book is a must.**"
—*Barbara Brennan*

Pathwork Press, 1994.
ISBN 0-9614777-4-1
$17.95

The Pathwork books are available at your local bookstore.

Pathwork Press
1355 Stratford Court #16
Del Mar, California 92014
ph (619) 793-1246 fax (619) 259-5224
e-mail: PathPress@aol.com